Symposium on Creation V

Symposium on Creation V

Edited by
Donald W. Patten

BAKER BOOK HOUSE
Grand Rapids, Michigan

Two of the articles in this volume have already appeared in print. "Galileo and the Church: Tensions with a Message for Today," by T. H. Leith, was published in four parts in the Journal of the American Scientific Affiliation 25 *(1973). "Evolution: the Ocean Says No!" by Stuart E. Nevins, is number eight in the Institute for Creation Research's* Impact Series. *Both are being reprinted by permission.*

Contents

List of Contributors

W. DENNIS BURROWES is the assistant director of the Provincial Department of Health's Division of Vital Statistics, Victoria, British Columbia. He is also North American secretary of the Evolution Protest Movement, founded in England in 1932. Previously he served the government of his native Jamaica as agricultural statistician, agricultural economist, and director of statistics. He has studied at Wolmer's School, Jamaica; Oxford University, England (M.A. with honors in agricultural science); and Rothamsted, England (postgraduate studies in statistics). Burrowes was elected Fellow of the Royal Statistical Society in 1950. He was born in 1918.

BOLTON DAVIDHEISER has been professor of biology at both Westmont and Biola colleges. He holds degrees from Swarthmore College (A.B.) and Johns Hopkins University (Ph.D.). He has held two research fellowships. Davidheiser contributed a monthly column, "Science and the Bible," to *Kings Business* for eleven years. He is author of *Evolution and the Christian Faith* (1969), *Science and the Bible* (1971), and "The Scopes Trial," an article which appeared in volume three of this series.

GORDON HOLMES FRASER is chancellor of Southwestern School of Missions, an institution which he founded and which combines an Indian Bible institute, a Navajo language school, and a missionary training school. It is located in Flagstaff, Arizona. He has studied at University of Oregon, University of California, California Baptist Theological Seminary, and Northern Arizona University (B.S. in anthropology, M.A. in the teaching of English as a second lan-

7

guage). Born in Quebec in 1898, Fraser has made a lifetime study of primitive religions and tribal languages.

T. H. LEITH teaches at York University, Toronto, specializing in the history of science. He previously taught at Gordon College and University of Rhode Island. He has studied at University of Toronto (B.A. with honors in physics and geology); Boston University (M.S. in geophysics, Ph.D. in philosophy of science); the Massachusetts Institute of Technology. Leith helped found the *Gordon Review* (now the *Christian Scholar's Quarterly*) and has published several articles in the *Journal of the American Scientific Affiliation* on various aspects of the philosophy of science. He was born in Toronto.

STUART E. NEVINS is assistant professor of geology at Christian Heritage College in El Cajon, California, and serves on the staff of the Institute for Creation Research. He holds the B.S. and M.S. in geology. Nevins has published articles in volumes two and three of this series, in ICR's *Acts and Facts,* and in *Creation Research Society Quarterly.*

LOREN C. STEINHAUER is a theorist for Mathematical Sciences Northwest, Seattle. He was previously instructor in applied mathematics at Massachusetts Institute of Technology and before that an acting assistant professor of aeronautics and astronautics at University of Washington, where he earned the B.S., M.S., and Ph.D. degrees. His doctorate is in aeronautics and astronautics and his dissertation was entitled, "Laser Heating of a Stationary Plasma." One of his published articles appeared in volume four of this series. He was born in Oregon in 1944.

ROBERT L. WHITELAW is professor of mechanical and nuclear engineering at Virginia Polytechnic Institute and State University and is also doing research in suspended vehicle systems and geothermal power generation. He has studied at University of Toronto (graduate degree with honors in engineering physics) and, during twenty-five years as a practicing engineer, at National Gas Turbine Establishment in England, Oak Ridge School of Reactor Technology, and U.S. Naval Postgraduate School. Whitelaw was in the forefront of many pioneer developments in jet propulsion, supercritical power generation, direct conversion and atomic energy. He has authored many technical reports and owns many patents. He was born of missionary parents in China in 1917.

Foreword

The lead article in this, the fifth volume of the series, is certainly one of the most outstanding in the entire series. Gordon Fraser's "The Gentile Names of God" is a linguistic analysis of words meaning "God" or "deity" in aboriginal and ancient languages from six continents, and it concludes that most of them have a common root or are phonetically related. Fraser's research is careful in detail and breath-taking in scope. It is also pregnant with implications, for if his conclusions are sound, the evolution of religions is impossible. Fraser's work should open the way for more, and potentially exciting, linguistic analysis by other motivated, alert creation scientists.

"What is wrong with carbon 14 dating?" is a question often sincerely asked creationists. Robert Whitelaw answers it in "The Testimony of Radiocarbon to the Genesis Flood." Slowly, or perhaps suddenly, the light dawns: nothing at all is wrong with carbon 14 dating—if only researchers and writers have a catastrophic world view, admitting sedimentary deposition on a global scale, both near to and far from present sea level. This transforms seeming contradictions between the Bible and science into points of agreement and argues strongly for creation science and catastrophism.

Stuart Nevins also discusses sedimentation, although in terms of gross volume rather than carbon 14 composition. In "Evolution: The Ocean Says No," he presents compelling evidence for catastrophism and against uniformitarianism.

Five centuries of scientific discovery—some of it more speculation than discovery—and reactions to it have been logged in the Western world. The first major breakthroughs must be credited to Copernicus and Kepler, both Germans and men of faith, men of science who viewed God as a maker of moral and religious laws as well as

natural laws. Harry Leith spans the eras of Copernicus and of
Kepler and Galileo in "Galileo and the Church: Tensions with a
Message for Today." Here are some important lessons for alert
creation students and teachers. The history of Christian leadership
has been spotty, what with its Newtons and its Burnets, its Pasteurs
and its Darwins. Reactions have sometimes been very good, sometimes sad, sometimes silly. Men of faith have sometimes responded
with remarkable foresight.

Loren Steinhauer is a catastrophist as well as a mathematician and
physicist, and he has a broad background in Bible history. Looking
at both from the perspective of astronomy, he argues against uniformitarianism in "Tracing the Past: Is Uniformity Meaningful?"
and for its opposite in "The Case for Global Catastrophism."

Bolton Davidheiser's biographical essay, "Gregor Mendel," is the
first such essay in this series of volumes, but we intend to include one
in each future volume. Davidheiser reviews Mendel's background as
a teacher in the Catholic educational system of central Europe, his
remarkable experimentation, his discovery of the laws of inheritance, and his being overlooked by the scientific community of his
day. This essay should broaden the perspective of creationist students and teachers.

Dennis Borrowes, an agricultural scientist whose studies included
genetics, examines the biblical story of Jacob and Laban in "Genetics
and Jacob's Flock," applying principles of inheritance of coat color
and character in livestock.

This is a variety of materials from creationist authors, men of faith
who are also men of science. It is a choir of many voices, a symphony
of many sounds that will thrill the student of nature and of the works
of God. Some data comes from the rocks, some from the heavens,
some from masterfully-designed biological structures, some from
ancient history, and some from more recent history. Some of the
information is practical and some theoretical. Some essays stress
assumptions, others conclusions. Here is the testimony of well-
trained men who appreciate and understand something of the mag-
nificence and majesty of the Creator.

DONALD W. PATTEN

1

The Gentile Names of God

Gordon Holmes Fraser

One of the most unavoidable problems faced by evolutionists at the turn of the century was that of the origin of religion. If the concept of evolution was valid, religion must also have evolved. Andrew Lang, the Scottish ethnologist and folklorist who was one of the evolutionists' most vocal antagonists, defined their problem:

> Variously stated by Darwin, Huxley, Mr. Herbert Spencer, and the manual-makers, the current hypothesis is this; beginning with the idea of human souls, or ghosts, and their propitiation, mankind, by ascending the steps of fetishes, departmental gods, nature gods, and polytheism generally, climbed to a conception of a Supreme Being. The advance of society to aristocracy and monarchy made it natural to imagine a heavenly Olympian aristocracy—the higher gods of polytheism—or a supreme being, a sort of heavenly king. In its earlier savage stages according to the hypothesis, religion is non-moral, lending little or no sanction to ethics.
>
> Now if some of the lowest or most backward races of mankind are found to possess a faith in a moral, beneficient, powerful being, whose home is above the heavens, though these races neither sacrifice to ghosts, nor bow to kings, nor believe in departmental gods, nor in the nature-gods of polytheism, it is clear that the friends of the theory of Huxley, Darwin, Tylor and Spencer are in a quandary. For here, among these low savages, is a god where no god should be. Here is the effect—a relatively supreme being—without the alleged causes, ghost worship, polytheism, aristocratic and monarchial society, worship of nature gods, and all the rest.[1]

Anthropologists, working with primitive tribes in a number of world areas and unaware of each other's findings, were reporting with a

1. "Are Savage Gods Borrowed from Missionaries?" *The Nineteenth Century* (January 1899), p. 132.

striking coincidence the concept of a Supreme Being among supposedly primitive peoples. Researchers termed these supreme beings sky-gods or high-gods, since without exception they were considered to live "in the sky," "behind the sun," or, as some of the
jungle tribes believed, "above the tree tops." These field researchers
also invariably found a lower level of religion, the appeasement of
troublesome spirits inhabiting the local scene; it involved cult and
ritual, including shamanistic exorcism. Creationists would insist that
these contrasting levels of religious practice and lofty belief are quite
in keeping with the apostle Paul's thesis in Romans 1:18-28: men
originally knew the one God but degenerated to polytheism, fetishism, and animism.

The facts reported by researchers among the tribes were most
damaging to the evolutionary concept, but its proponents continued
to develop theories of the origin and evolution of religion.

For example, Sir Edward B. Tylor proposed that religion began
with animism. The primitive savage assumed that the animate organism surrounding him must also be possessed of a spirit. The
savage concluded that, while he dreamed, a conscious part of him
left his body and went on a journey; thus he conceived of a "soul." If
his soul failed to return from one of its "journeys," he would, of
course, die.

Emilé Durkheim saw totemism and a collectivist form of worship
as the keys. His "minimum definition of religion implies an an-
tithesis of the Sacred and the Profane, and the union of fellow-
worshippers of the sacred in a sort of church."[2] He believed their
ideas of the sacred to be surrounded by totemic ritualism; thus,
totemism represents the essence of archaic religion.

Sir James Frazer proposed that the performance of rites of magic
constituted the beginnings of religion. The shaman, with his rituals
of imitative and contagious magic, his fetishes, and his spells, is the
priest of the tribe's religion.[3]

B. Spencer and F. J. Gillen, researchers in Australia, proposed
naturalism: man, seeing the forces of nature (storm, lightning,
flood, etc.) as sinister, had his priests perform rituals to appease
these forces.[4]

Adherents of the evolutionary doctrines that were taking the
academic world by storm were willing to accept any of these theories,

2. Robert Lowie, *Primitive Religion* (New York: Grossett and Dunlap, 1952), p. 153.
Lowie analyzes both the totemism of Durkheim and the animism of Tylor and
compares the two.

3. *The Golden Bough*, 13 vols. (New York: St. Martin's, n.d.). Condensed by Theodore
H. Gaster, *The New Golden Bough* (New York: Mentor, 1964).

4. *The Native Tribes of Central Australia* (London, 1899); *The Northern Tribes of Central
Australia* (London, 1904).

or a synthesis of all of them, as long as this would provide a scheme of religious origins compatible with their doctrines.

Unfortunately for all concerned, only a sampling of savage tribes had been more than superficially studied, hardly enabling anthropologists to see beyond the ubiquitous cultic ritual and magical appeasement; they tended to interpret the various rituals, often colorful and apparently filled with symbolism, as the sum total of the tribe's religious belief and practice. Later, however, more persistent and painstaking investigators, after gaining the confidence of the tribes, almost always uncovered a higher level of religious thought, a cosmogony that acknowledged a Creator and Sustainer who, being a spirit, could not be pictured, sculpted, or pantomimed by a human actor. In many cases, quite valid prayers were offered to this Supreme Being. As such field investigation increased, so did the number of tribes believing in the existence of the "high-gods."

During the first half of the present century, the research of the past hundred years was exhaustively collated and studied by Father Dr. Wilhelm Schmidt in his six-volume, 4,500-page classic, *Der Ursprung der Gottesidee* (1934). Schmidt pays tribute to Andrew Lang for his valiant effort to bring before the public the facts of the matter in a day when it was almost intellectual suicide to oppose the doctrine of evolution and its high priests:

> Andrew Lang . . . had been a champion of the animist theory of Tylor, but he discovered that this, as well as the manistic theory of Spencer, either disregarded or denied sufficient consideration to the supreme being found among many, and especially most primitive peoples, whose being and essence does not accord with those theories. It was just at that time, through the discoveries of Howitt in southeastern Australia, that a number of such supreme beings had been brought to light from among the oldest Australian peoples. On the basis of these findings, Lang published a criticism of Tylor's theory in his volume *The Making of Religion* (1898). The theory which he here sets forth defends the possibility that primitive man, from a consideration of the cosmic forces, was capable of arriving at a knowledge of a Supreme Being as Creator, Preserver of the world, and Lawgiver to man. Lang contends that this Being is apprehended prior to formation of the explicit idea of soul, because it is designated as a person absolutely, before there is any distinction of body and soul; therefore the animist theory missed the mark on this score from the start.
>
> As proof Lang points to a series of primitive peoples, for example, the southeastern Australians, the Andaman Islanders, the Bantu and Sudan Negroes, and several North American tribes, among whom the veneration, or at least the acknowledgment, of such Supreme Beings has been demonstrated beyond doubt, even before the advent of Europeans or missionaries.[5]

5. *Primitive Revelation*, trans. Joseph J. Baierl (St. Louis: R. Herder, 1939), pp. 120, 121.

Dr. Schmidt insists that the closer we get to the few representatives of the primary herding cultures, the purer the concept of the high-god. "There remains one of the primary cultures, that of the pastoral nomads, the great cattle breeding people. These are still to be found in their natural state, their representatives being Altaic or Ural-Altaic and Hamitic races . . . in their natural state, however, the great cattle-breeding peoples display a quite characteristic form of religion, not to be found in this particular shape in any other cultures. They steadfastly believe in and worship a supreme sky-god."[6] Speaking of remote tribes generally placed at the bottom of the ladder of primitiveness, Schmidt says: "In the primitive cultures, we have before us a number of tribes in which no deities, or very few, appear at the side of the Supreme Being. This is the case with the Pygmys of French Gaboon, the Negritos in the Philippines, the Kurnai in southeast Australia, the Fuegians. Among the Algonquin and Salish in north-central California such deities are found, but they are created by the Supreme Being and subject to Him."[7]

Schmidt, a competent theologian as well as ethnologist but writing from a historian's viewpoint rather than a biblicist's, agrees with the apostle Paul's schedule of deterioration of religious worship. The casual or untrained observer, on the other hand, tends to overlook evidences of the high-god in the mythologies and rituals, especially as the tribe retreats from its basic primitivism and its rituals obscure its nobler beliefs. Schmidt recognizes this.

> In proportion as we withdraw from the most primitive peoples and approach the semi-civilized ones, these three elements, magic, ghost worship and nature worship, take deeper root and finally overrun the ancient veneration of the Supreme Being to such a degree as to render it no longer visible.[8]

He insists that the attributes of the high-god in tribal concepts are those of the Supreme Being in the great ethnic religions.

> It is not only the faculty of concentrated thought which it implies, that this monotheism shows the high estimation we may give to the religion of these primitive peoples. For its Supreme Being Himself is, in the fullness of His attributes and functions, an ideal personification of the highest essential and moral character, and well calculated to inspire the peoples that acknowledge and honor Him with the high value of active life and solemn moral virtue.
>
> Heaven is His dwelling place; in early times He was usually on earth among men, but went away from them on account of a sin of theirs. Thus He is a person in heaven. It is this dwelling place of His that

6. *The Origin and Growth of Religion* (New York: Dial, 1931), pp. 167, 168.

7. *Primitive Revelation,* p. 125.

8. Ibid., p. 123.

often suggests the names given Him: "He who is above," "The Old One above," "The Heavenly One." The actual term, "Heaven" is used only by one branch, the Samoyeds, however, they are already passing over to the primary culture of nomadic herders, where this name became general.[9]

The persistence of reports from field anthropologists of the worship of sky-gods by tribes considered the most primitive could not help but irritate evolutionary writers. It was not logical that some tribes should ascend from animism and totemism to monotheism and other tribes equally primitive deteriorate from monotheism to animism. Tylor, who shares an equal place with Darwin and Lyell, admits this problem in a book originally published in 1881:

> It is necessary for the student to be alive to the importance of decline in civilization, but it is here more particularly mentioned in order to point out that it in no way contradicts the theory that civilization itself is developed from low to high stages. One cannot lose a thing without having had it first, and wherever tribes are fallen from a higher civilization of their ancestors, this only leaves it to be accounted for how that higher civilization grew up.
>
> On the whole it appears that wherever there are found elaborate arts, abstruse knowledge, complex institutions, these are results of gradual development from an earlier simpler and ruder state of life. No stage of civilization comes into existence spontaneously, but grows or is developed out of the stage before it.[10]

Tylor makes the mistake of most cultural anthropologists when he assumes that the advance of religious forms and rituals should parallel the advance of the arts and civilization, and that an elaborate ritualism replete with symbolism represents religion at its highest. To the contrary, history demonstrates that the religion of advanced civilizations, like that of Ur of the Chaldees when Abraham and his family left, was corrupt and decadent despite its elaborate ceremonies and despite the high level of the civilization's arts and economic life.

Anthropologists would classify Abraham the Semite a nomadic primitive, whose only religious paraphernalia was a butcher knife for slaying his offerings and a pile of stones for an altar. But Abraham, unlike the priests of Ur, had a personal relationship with Jehovah; thus, worship at its simplest is worship at its profoundest.

Of those who defended creationist doctrine during the controversy, only a few wrote specifically about the presence of the

---

9. Ibid., p. 125.

10. *Anthropology* (Ann Arbor: University of Michigan, 1960), p. 13. Tylor applied the theory of evolution to culture and religion and Lyell applied it to geology; their combined efforts provided the long period of time essential to Darwin's theory of organic evolution.

knowledge of God. Lang wrote voluminously in the public press
(with the evolutionists writing equally voluminous rebuttals) and
authored three books in which he stated the facts.[11] The first full-
length treatment, written by Dio Pettazzoi, did not appear until
1922.[12] G. Foucart wrote a full-scale article on the universality of the
presence of the high-god for the *Encyclopedia of Religion and Ethics.*
Foucart says that the high-god

> occupies the same place in the semi-civilized religions of Pre-
> Columbian America as we find in all groups of so-called non-civilized
> religions without exception. We may safely presume that the concept
> of sky-god belongs to the most ancient period in the history of reli-
> gious feeling, and that it is at least as ancient as primitive naturism and
> animistic fetishism. Whether it is even pre-animist in its fundamental
> aspect is a question which must be reserved in the meantime.
>
> The nature, role and characteristics of this universal sky-god may
> be concealed under the most diverse forms, but he is always more or
> less recognizable to the historian of religions and always identical in
> essential definition. America shows him in the mythology of the
> Toltecs, the Mayas and the Incas as well as in Brazil, in the Andes,
> among the Caribs, in Tierra del Fuego, and at the extreme north
> among the Eskimos.
>
> The sky-god has reigned everywhere; his kingdom still covers the
> whole of the uncivilized world. No historical or proto-historical mo-
> tive can be assigned as a cause, and neither the migrations of races nor
> the diffusion of myths and folk-lore affords the slightest justification
> of the fact. The universality of the sky-god and the uniformity of his
> essential characteristics are the logical consequences of the constant
> uniformity of the primitive system of cosmogony.[13]

The same encyclopedia contains many other references to the subject, also.

When the controversy was at its height, the evolutionists did
everything possible to eradicate the idea. They ignored the subject
in their writings and especially in textbooks—scarcely a college or
high-school text refers to the concept; and they insisted that,
whenever a high level of religion appears in a pagan tribe, it is a
product of missionary influence. Schmidt virtually accuses the
anthropologists of suppressing the facts:

> It is obvious that the fundamental change which set in about this
> time (1890-1910) both in ethnology and in general attitude of Euro-

11. Besides his articles in *The Nineteenth Century* and in *The Contemporary Review* (the
most notable being "The Evolution of the Idea of God," 1898), Lang authored *Myth,
Literature and Religion* (1887), *Magic and Religion* (1901), and *The Making of Religion*
(1896).

12. *Formazione a Sviluppo del Monoteismo Nelle Storia del Religioni* (Milan, 1922).

13. "Sky Gods, Universality and Antiquity," in *Encyclopedia of Religion and Ethics,* 13
vols., ed. James Hastings (New York: Scribner's, 1908-1927), 11:580.

pean educated thought had a not inconsiderable share in preventing this theory of the Supreme sky-god in primitive times from reaching its full development. . . . This change which began for ethnology, as early as Lubbock, and was completed by Spencer and Tylor, was a new interest in savage races.

Such a change would not in itself have sufficed to kill the theory of the sky-god so completely; for among savages also such a supreme deity is widely distributed. But the doctrine of progressive evolution, which was then being put forward from the most various quarters and soon mastered the mind of all Europe, necessarily brought about such a result if it was understood and developed in a materialistic spirit as was then the case. Under this twofold influence all framers of theories concerning fetishes, ghosts, animism, totemism and magic, if they agreed in nothing else were at one in this, that the figure of the sky-god must be got rid of from the earliest stages of religion, as being too high and incomprehensible. For, as they held, these savages must have been extremely low, not far removed from the beasts; therefore the sky-god must be referred to quite late stages of development, unless it was preferred to deduce him from Christian influences.

The strength of this unusual current of thought was so great, and the resulting discredit into which it brought the notion of the great age of the sky-god so complete, that hardly anyone found courage to oppose it and to draw attention to the quite frequent examples of this exalted sky-god appearing among decidedly primitive peoples, where not the least trace of Christian influence was to be found.[14]

While studying evidences of pre-Christian theism among the Salish tribes on the Pacific Northwest coast in the 1930s, the author faced the following basic questions regarding the identity of the high-gods:

1. Were their attributes sufficiently uniform and comprehensive to warrant the hypothesis that their worshipers once knew the one true God and that this knowledge deteriorated through the centuries to the point that each individual tribe believed its high-god unique?

2. If they were, is there in the written history and mythology of ancient peoples, apart from the biblical record and the documents of the great ethnic religions, an indication that one supreme God was revered?

3. If there is, is there also a free morpheme used as a proper name, or a bound morpheme used as an affix in agglutinative or polysynthetic word clauses, or a generic root that serves as a base for common nouns or sacred elements?[15]

14. *Origin and Growth,* pp. 170, 171.

15. A *morpheme* is any word or part of a word, an affix or combining form, that conveys meaning and that cannot be divided into parts that also convey meaning; its meaning, even in various contexts, is relatively stable. *Bake* is a free morpheme; *er* is a bound morpheme, meaningless by itself but meaningful when suffixed to *bake.*

It was obvious that an affirmative answer to the third question also would settle the first two. Answering it would involve a study of the earliest written records, which philologists and anthropologists generally date in the fourth millennium B.C. These writings are inscribed on clay tablets, some of which were located below the flood level in Mesopotamia.[16]

The Origin of Language

No one would question the assumption that language was spoken before it was written. Creationists do question the assumption, however, that the development of language required thousands of years, during which primitives grunted and gestured, imitating bird calls, the sounds of other animals, and the sounds of everyday living in the ancestral cave. Of course, man's language grew as he experienced and observed more things, but creationists believe that man was created with the ability to express himself verbally.

Languages and dialects would obviously result from migrations and, after a few generations of isolation from the original clan-groups, the language of a group would show definite changes. Written language would be invented (probably by a single individual) within a single generation, as soon as it became necessary to record history or keep family records, or as soon as commercial and social interests demanded it. Any normal individual today could invent a written language within a reasonably short time, and while we have greater technical skill, we are no smarter than those who helped form languages or develop written codes.

Written languages undoubtedly developed contemporaneously with the dialects and new spoken languages.

Language undoubtedly started simply and expanded rapidly as the waves of migration moved out from the nuclear area, prompted by mounting pressures. The biblical statement that at one time the whole earth spoke one language (Gen. 11:1) is quite in keeping with the known facts of language expansion. Evolutionists have, on general principles, fought the monogenetic theory of language. They either reject or avoid discussion of Friedrich Müller's (and Darwin's) theory that the "speech" of animals must have developed gradually into human speech, preferring instead to speak of the "miracle" of language.[17] Margaret Schlauch writes: "Today most authors are extremely cautious when they touch upon the unrecoverable epoch when speech originated. They will avoid committing themselves on the question as to whether this happened

16. P. J. Wiseman, *New Discoveries in Babylonia About Genesis* (London: Marshall, Morgan and Scott, n.d.), pp. 24-26.

17. Richard Albert Wilson, *The Miraculous Birth of Language* (New York: Philosophical Library, n.d.).

once or several times in various parts of the world. In any case, they say, the answer is unimportant, even irrelevant, for the solution of problems significant for us today."[18] After discussing Alfredo Trombetti's forceful and exhaustive arguments for monogenesis,[19] Schlauch concludes, "The question about a single origin for the diverse tongues of mankind must be tabled until we know more of their earlier forms; and that may be—forever."[20]

Linguistic research has refined the evidence for monogenesis. The languages of the American Indians are one example. In 1910 a United States government report identified 294 tribes of American Indians and fifty-four language stocks or families. Research has reduced fifty-four to six or seven, and linguists admit that these families could be classified as a common type.[21] Indo-Aryan languages are another example. European philologists of the last century showed that these languages came from a single source, which Franz Bopp spoke of as the *Stammsprache*. These philologists furnished additional evidence for the monogenetic origin of language when they isolated the Hamito-Semitic and Sinitic families. Linguistic science has been unable to push back the emergence of written language any further than 3500 B.C., and its only source book for the origin of spoken language is the Bible.

Biblicists date the explosion of languages between the Noachian Deluge and the building of the Tower of Babel. Erich Sauer explains the event logically and scientifically:

> The confounding of language is in the first instance something fourfold; a confounding of vocabulary, grammar, pronunciation and phraseology, and in this sense there are today about a thousand languages and chief dialects. Yet it is something further.
>
> Whatever the original language may been been, whether (as the rabbis and church fathers supposed) the Hebrew or Aramaic or (which is no doubt alone right) none of the old languages handed down to us, in any case the community of speech involved a vigorous uniformity of mental life. For because language is the phonetic manifestation of the mental, the mental part of all mankind must in a special sense have been uniform so long as its expression, language, was uniform.
>
> The confusion of tongues was thus at the same time a confusing of the basic mental conceptions of mankind, since, through an act of God's power upon the human spirit, in place of the original oneness

18. *The Gift of Language* (New York: Dover, 1955), p. 73.

19. *L'unita d'Origine del Linguaggio, Saggi Glottologia Generale Comparata* (Bologna, 1920); *Elementi di Glottologia* (Bologna, 1923).

20. *Gift of Language*, p. 74.

21. U.S. Department of Commerce, Bureau of Census, *Indian Population in the United States and Alaska* (Washington, D.C.: Government Printing Office, 1915).

there set in a manifold cleavage in thought, feeling, and idea. Hence every language has its own linguistic "spirit." Thus the confusion of tongues became at the same time a confusion of thought and conception.[22]

Development from the line drawings of the first proto-cuneiform tablets to the explosion of writing and speech represented by the wide range of pictographic Chinese and Egyptian and then to syllabic and alphabetic forms of Phoenician, Greek, and proto-Hebrew required no more than 1,500 years.

The continuity of language represented in the proliferation of clay tablets and the inscriptions of monuments, dating from before the Noachian Deluge, provides the required basis for studying the inventory of words and ideas that were used to express even philosophic concepts such as the person and attributes of Deity. We can expect, too, to find the written record that will substantiate the contention that the high-gods of the world's peoples were known when language and religious thought emerged.

We who speak a western European language are more conscious of the heritage and diffusion of the Indo-European or Indo-Aryan language family and can cite examples of the evolution of words in different languages from a single stem. When we hear a Dane or Swede say *fisk*, a German *fisch*, a Hollander *visch*, a Breton *pesk*, or an Englishman *fish*, we have no difficulty in tracing them all to their Gothic ancestor *fisks*.

The philologists of the past century—Max Müller, Delbrück, Franz Bopp, and Sir William Jones—did yeoman service in tracing the languages of Europe, Persia, and India back to their sources. Jones first noted that the Sanscritic-based languages of India had a close kinship to his native English as well as to Latin and Greek: "The Sanskrit language, whatever may be its antiquity, is of wonderful structure; more perfect than Greek, more copious than Latin, and more exquisitely refined than either; yet bearing to both of them a stronger affinity, both in the roots of the verbs and in the forms of grammar, than could have been produced by accident; so strong that no philologer could examine all the three without believing them to have sprung from some common source."[23] And Bopp, when he started reading Ulfilas' Gothic New Testament,[24] thought he was

---

22. *Dawn of World Redemption* (Grand Rapids: Eerdmans, 1952), pp. 81, 82.

23. Quoted in B. Delbrück, *Introduction to the Study of Language*, trans. E. Channing (London, 1882), p. 1.

24. Ulfilas, appointed missionary bishop to the Goths in A.D. 341, reduced Gothic to writing and translated the Scriptures into that language. The Gothic version of the Bible is the only extant example of fourth-century Gothic.

reading Sanskrit. He spoke of an ancestral language which no longer exists but from which individual languages were derived.[25]

Knowledge of ancient Mediterranean languages which has been acquired since the time of Bopp and Jones takes us back in history and language lore almost to the Tower of Babel and the explosion of languages.

Original Names of God

In the earliest stages of written language, a single written symbol did duty for several phonetic values, and in some cases a single symbol represented synonyms, the immediate context indicating which word was intended. The symbol for Deity, for example, expressed both ideas and phonetic values.

In the oldest known line-written precuneiform tablets, which antedate the Deluge, *God* is written with a triad of stars. This was later simplified to a single star. Then as cuneiform emerged and became stylized, the star was written with the cuneo stroke of a stylus. As the cuneiform script expanded its inventory of written symbols, the star was simplified further to a cross, then to a simpler cross, and finally to a single horizontal stroke (fig. 1).[26]

The symbol expressed, in addition to "God," "light," "day," "heaven," "brightness," and, as ancestor veneration developed and monarchies were established, "king," "deified ancestors," "hero."

As the attributes of Deity were distinguished, the same symbol was used for *El*, the Almighty; *JH*, The Eternal; and *Ti*, the Most High, a term used later, and comprehensively, as the Gentile name of God. In all cases the context indicated which term was meant.

As tribal languages and dialects emerged, new phonetic values were expressed by the same symbol, and this trend continued as long as the cuneiform script was used in Sumerian, Hittic, Ugaritic,

25. *Study of Language,* p. 131.

26. Rudolph E. Brünnow, *A Classified List of Simple and Compound Ideographs* (Leyden, 1897), p. 26.

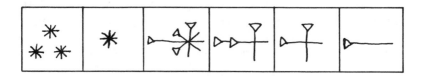

Fig. 1. The earliest symbols for *God*

Chaldean and Babylonian, and Old Persian. C. J. Ball writes that "the character ⊶⊤, an 'high,' 'heaven,' anu, 'The God of Heaven,' which was read dingir in the sense of a god also meant Ia'u or Ya'u and Ia-a-ti or Ya-ti. The latter is the Assyrian first person pronoun . . . and may well be the prototype for the Semite first personal pronoun."[27] He also suggests that Ia'u and Ya'u are the predecessors of the final form of the Hebrew JHVH.[28]

Ball also gives a clue to the development of the name of God among the Ural-Altaic, Turkic, Samoyed peoples. Their names for God vary only slightly and within a dialectic pattern: Tengri (Kalmuck), Tengeri (Buriat), Tangere (Tatar), Tangara (Yakut and Dolgan). Mongolian folklore speaks of the Blue Tengri and the Eternal Tengri. A striking coincidence is the name Tangaroa, one of the names of God in the South Pacific archipelagoes. When the term is reduced to its dominant phonemes, the similarity is even more evident. The phonemes /d/ or /t/, /n/, /g/ and /r/ are the same. Vowel sounds vary with dialects and the added vowels in the South Pacific forms are a requirement of the Polynesian and Melanesian languages. More will be said on this when we study the area in question.

As is the case in most languages the same term also accommodates the common noun for gods and ancestors as well as for the sky itself. Ball says: "The ordinary Sumerian term for 'god,' Dingir, Digir, dimir is written ⊶⊤, which in the oldest form of the script appears as a single star, while mul (⊶⊤) is a group of three stars. Not only so, the word ⊶⊤ (digir, etc.) is recorded to have meant kakkabu, 'star' as well as ilu, 'god.' See Tab. 5R 21539 while Tab. C T XXI 4 adds to these meanings ellu, 'bright,' 'pure' (equals El-Supreme). The reason for these applications of the word lies in the fact that digir is an intensive compound, meaning something like 'bright flashing'; made up of di, 'to sparkle' or 'glitter' (nabtu) and gir, 'lightning,' 'to flash.' "[29] The term persists in Turkish in connection with the worship of heaven. M. A. Czaplika writes, "Sacrifice to the sky, tigir, is one of the most persistent ceremonies among the old and modern Turks and is performed every third summer."

A single root word, Di or Ti, can be isolated in languages and language families worldwide. It is a language factor or morpheme which indicates: (1) the name of God, (2) a common noun for deities, (3) sacred concepts, (4) an honorific for ancestors or kings. The morpheme is present in the first recorded phonetic expressions of the early clay tablets (c. 3000 B.C.), and is still turning up when previously untranslated languages are being reduced to writing.

27. *Sumer and Shem* (New York: Oxford University, 1915), pp. 14, 15.

28. Ibid., p. 32.

29. Ibid., p. 9.

This language factor is present as a complete word in isolating languages like Chinese and inflectional languages like English. It is found as a prefix, suffix, or infix in agglutinative languages like Finnish and Navajo and polysynthetic languages like Algonquin. This is certainly solid evidence that the factor was disseminated worldwide from a common source, and at a time when the languages of the world were making their first transition from the *Stammsprache* of Franz Bopp and B. Delbrück, and when the tribes of the world were starting to migrate.

The presence of the morpheme in the American Indian languages is evidence that these tribes brought the word with them from the old world at a date late enough to demonstrate that variations were already developing, variations that would be expected as peoples break up into tribes and nations.

A ready demonstration of the dispersion of the root word or morpheme is the Indo-European family of languages. Unthinkingly we use *deity* as a generic term to express the concept of the Supreme God as well as *gods.*

Deity draws on a Latin word *deus,* which immediately suggests, for instance, the Italian *Dio,* French *Dieu,* Spanish *Dios,* Old Irish *Dia,* Welsh *Duw,* Breton *Doue,* Lithuanian *Dievas,* Lettish *Dieus,* Sanskrit *Dyu,* Greek *Theos,* Catalonian *Deu,* Cornish *Dew,* Gaelic *Dia.*

God may seem unrelated but is in fact related to the German *Gött,* and the Danish and Swedish *Gud,* etc. An apparently unrelated variation used in the Slavic languages is represented by the Russian *Bog,* Czech-Slovak *Bogu,* Serb-Croatian *Bog,* Avestan (India) *Baga,* etc.

God is descended from northern India where *KhuDa* is used in the Brahui dialect in Baluchistan, the Musalmani dialect in Punjabi, and the Urdu of Hindustani. *Hudah* is a variant used in the Balochi dialect of Baluchistan. An ancient variant close to the original is *Gu ti,* the high-god of the Gutians, the mountaineer tribe that conquered Sumer and Akkad c. 2230 B.C. and remained in power for a century.[30] They later spread from Armenia to Persia. They were probably identical to the ancient Qurti, the predecessors of the modern Kurds.

The Kirghis of the Asian steppes used *Kudai* as the name of the high-god; the ancient Persians used *Hudai,* which suggests an ancient relationship between the two peoples. Solomon C. Malan relates these two words to the English *God:* "A satisfactory reason for the use of 'God,' without the article, lies . . . in the meaning of the word itself. It is akin to *Khuda* or *Khudai,* . . . and as a name which belongs to the Most High, like *Illati* and *Elillah,* [it] means 'a being

30. Hans G. Güterbock, "Babylonia and Assyria: History." *Encyclopaedia Britannica,* 24 vols. (Chicago: William Benton, 1970), 2:961.

who has brought himself into existence. . . . 'God' would probably be taken to mean 'self existent.' "[31]

The *Bog* of Russian, *Baga* of Avestan, *Buh* of Bohemian, etc., are also from an Aryan word, *Bhaga,* of the Urartian-Armenian-Slavic chain of development. We find, for instance, the Kurkus using *Bag Da* as their name for the Most High God. *The Encyclopedia of Religion and Ethics* informs us that "the Kurkus (west central India) worship *Bagh* or *Vagh Deo* . . . who pretends to know spells by which he can protect himself and his parishioners from the beast (tiger)."[32]

The Balahis and other tribes in west central India know both the *Bhagda* and the *Khudai.* "*Bhagwan* . . . is also called *Paramatma* (supreme Spirit), *Parmeshwar* (Supreme God), *Ishwar* (God), *Khuda* (name of God used by Mohammedans). *Bhagwan* comes nearest to the concept of God of the monotheistic religions. The Balahis clearly distinguish the *deas* and *matas.* They do not identify *Bhagwan* with any of the Hindu triad, *Brahma, Beshnu, Makesh,* as they call them. They maintain that these are the creatures of *Bhagwan.* . . . They believe that *Bhagwan* has a distinct personality, is eternal, without father or mother."[33]

Very early in the migrations of mankind after the Noachian Deluge, the predecessors of the Chinese apparently traveled eastward from the nuclear area of tribal beginnings. They apparently migrated about the time that the transition was being made from picture scripts to syllabic and alphabetical scripts. Instead of developing an alphabet, they retained their pictographic and ideographic forms, and their language became refined as a monosyllabic one in which each written symbol expresses an entire idea.

Ball finds parallels between the Sumerian and the Chinese which he considers an indication of a common time element and linguistic source: the Sumerian word meaning "month," *iti* or *itu,* is equivalent to the Chinese *uet;* the Sumerian word *ezen,* "festival," "fixed time," *isinnu,* compares with the Chinese *sun,* a period of seven or ten days.[34]

L. W. King suggests also a correspondence between the written forms. He cites a diorite statue of Gudea, Patesi of Shirpurla (*Louvre; Déc. en Chald. Pl. 14.*) which shows the early cuneiform symbols arranged in vertical columns much as Chinese symbols are arranged. These show the transitional form of *Ti* as ✳ instead of ✳ . In this inscription both cuneo stroke and the more ancient line writing is used. Several symbols in this inscription have a distinct

31. *Who Was God in China?* (London, c. 1895), p. 8.

32. 5:8.

33. Stephen Fuchs, *The Children of Hari* (Vienna, 1950), p. 228.

34. *Sumer and Shem,* p. 5.

resemblance to the Chinese characters. On the Blau monument (*Br. Mus. No. 86260*), the characters are written in vertical columns and the precuneiform character ✳ is used for *Ti*.[35]

Developed Names of God

China and East Asia. The Chinese can be said to be the only people who have existed as a literate nation, without interruption, through all the ages of recorded history. They carried a rudimentary literacy with them when they migrated to the valley of the Hwang Ho, and this literacy was refined and codified into a more or less permanent form within a few centuries of their existence as a homogenous people. It has not changed perceptibly during the forty-five centuries of Chinese history, and Sinologists today are able to decipher, with comparative ease, the inscriptions on the oracle bones.

Some will insist that the records of the first six centuries, from 1766 B.C. (Shang Dynasty) to 2356 B.C. (reign of Fu Hsi), are so mythical that they are without historical value. While it is true that much myth is woven into any ancient lore, it is also true that mythology is romanticized history. The basics are valid. It is a fact in favor of the reliability of this record that, less than one hundred years after Homer composed his *Iliad,* the writings of China had grown to such volume that Kung Fu Tzu was preparing an anthology of the literature of the fifteen centuries that had preceded his time. It is a known fact that libraries consisting of hundreds of thousands of volumes were in existence centuries before western Europeans began to emerge as civilized nations.

The fact that is important for our present study is that these migrants to the east carried with them the name and concept of the Most High God and so implanted it in their language and literature that the record has been continuous since writing began. Note that the first appearance in writing of the Chinese name for God the Most High antedates the first biblical use of the term (Gen. 14:18-22) by several hundred years.

Two names for God competed for supremacy in ancient China. Both are essentially correct, stemming from the same root, *Ti*. The Shang people insisted on the use of *Shang Ti*, whereas the Chow insisted on *T'ien*. Eventually *Shang Ti* designated the person of Deity and *T'ien*, heaven, His dwelling place.

> The Chinese language possesses two terms which, as far as etymology goes, seem adequate to stand for "God." The former of the two is *Shang Ti* or Sovereign (*Ti*) above (*Shang*); the second is *T'ien*, or heaven; often used in later centuries for the visible heavens, but explained in the ancient Han Dynasty dictionary as the Exalted in the highest, being formed of signs meaning the one who is great.

35. *History of Sumer and Akkad* (London, 1910), p. 66.

It is not lawful to use the name *Shang Ti* lightly, and therefore we name Him by His residence, which is *T'ien,* or heaven.

The earliest reference to *Shang Ti,* or indeed to any religion whatever, in the ancient history of China, is found in the words, "The yellow Emperor (2697-2598 B.C.) sacrificed to *Shang Ti,* gathered the whole populace together and diffused among them the principles of government and religion.[36]

The universal acceptance of *Shang Ti* is evidenced by its wide distribution throughout the many languages and dialects of China, as well as the languages of tribes within China's sphere of influence.

The written form of *Shang Ti* is always the same, but the spoken form varies slightly with each language and dialect. Thus *Shang Ti* in Mandarin is *Sheung Tai* in Cantonese, *Sing Di* in Hainanese, *Son Ti* among the Hakka of Kwangtung Province, *Shiong Doi* in Kien Ning, and *Zong Ti* in Tai Chow. There are probably as many as fifty variants of the spoken form.

Among other Asian people, more or less within China's sphere of influence, the Pnongs of Indochina use *N'du Chiong,* obviously a transposition of the Chinese term; the Kamhow dialect, spoken in the Chin Hills of Burma, uses *Shiang Tho;* and the Chungchi, a non-Chinese tribe living in Kweichou Province, uses *Sang Da.*

Probable uses of the term as a common noun include *Wati,* "king" in Lisu; *tuan* (which could be a loan word from the Chinese *t'ian* or the Sumerian *tian*), "chief" in Malay; and *du,* "chief" in the language of the Kachins.

Shinto, "The Way of the Gods" in Japanese, is undoubtedly borrowed from the Chinese. Other Japanese uses of the morpheme are: *Ta kama,* "The Plain of High Heaven"; *Diaboth,* a goddess; *Dai koku,* the god of both the rain and the artisans; and *Hotei,* the god of magnanimity.

The Japanese seem to have been theists originally rather than ancestor worshipers. A *Shinto* scholar, Atsutans Hirata (A.D. 1776-1843) says: "The object of fear and worship in foreign countries is known by several names; the Supreme Being, Sovereign Ruler, Imperial Heaven, or Heaven. He is none other than our Heavenly *Kami* who dwells in Heaven and governs all the affairs of the world."[37]

The Ainu, non-Japanese aborigines living on the island of Hokaido, are largely shamanistic and animistic; they have, however, a rudimentary knowledge of the Most High God. George C. Ring writes: "Ainu archaeology testifies to belief in survival after death but the findings throw no further light on the race's ancient religion.

36. *Encyclopedia of Religion and Ethics,* 6:272.

37. Quoted in *The Mythology of All Races,* ed. Louis Herbert Gray, 13 vols. (New York: Cooper Square, 1964), 8:48, 49.

Nowadays they acknowledge *Nis Ti,* a Supreme Being domiciled in the upper firmament. He is invoked in prayer on special occasions but since he is mysterious and remote and has committed mundane affairs to the *Kami* (spirits), these latter are the recipient of every day cult."[38]

The Koreans, certainly within the Chinese sphere of influence in classical times, have *Siang Tiei* as their Supreme God, obviously a use of the Chinese *Shang Ti.* The Koreans, like many others, use the root word as an affix in their names for deities; *Tigyama* is a protective deity of the home and *Tachue,* "Lord of the Place," is expected to avert evil and bring luck to the house.

Africa. The study of the knowledge of the Most High God on the continent of Africa can be a rewarding one. Probably no area of the world has had its native religions so closely observed, and the "dark continent" has been characterized, more than any other, as a land of witchcraft, shamanism, orgiastic rites, demon possession, and contagious and imitative magic. As is invariably the case, most observers have seen only the most dramatic religious excesses and have not inquired concerning a higher concept of the high-god.

Confirming that African tribes did have a knowledge of God is the fact that, when the Scriptures were translated into the native languages, almost without exception a satisfactory name was found for the Most High as Almighty, Creator, and Sustainer. In over 120 Scripture translations studied by this author, only one—the Gu or Dahomey—uses the term *Jiheyehe,* obviously a transliteration of the name Jehovah; and only nine—all from Islamic-dominated Sudan, Sierra Leone, French West Africa, and Nigeria—use a modification of *Allah.* All the others use colloquial terms, the most prominent of which are the *Mulungu, Mungu, Molongo* and the *Nzambi,* or variants of the Bantu languages.

The use of the universal root word for the Most High are infrequent, although cultural anthropologists have discovered some: *Ti xo* of the Kaffir in Basutoland; *Dyu* of the Bassa of Central Liberia; *Dyem* of the Angas Tribe of Nigeria's Bauchi Highlands; *Deban* of the Agoas of Abyssinia; and a deteriorated term, *Da,* the serpent god of Dahomey. Other likely instances are *Asiata* of the Nanda of the Africa Gold Coast; *Awondo* of the Munshi of Northern Nigeria; *Katonda* of the Boganda, a Bantu tribe of East Africa; and *Tilo,* the "dim mysterious power associated with the Sky," of the Thonga Tribe of South Africa.

Australia. The aboriginal Australians have challenged the imagination of anthropologists since first coming to their attention. They

38. *Religions of the Far East* (Milwaukee: Bruce, 1950), p. 76.

assumed that they had at last discovered the earth's most primitive
people who, because of their isolation, had been bypassed in their
evolutionary advance. A. L. Kroeber surmises that "the Native Australian culture . . . has been most nearly cut off and therefore remote from the continents during the tens or hundreds of thousands
of years that man and his culture have been spread over the
earth . . . it is sound in designating the Australian general level as
retarded by thousands of years behind the Eurasiatic . . . levels of
culture."[39]

The anthropologists thought they had surely found "fossil man,"
but thorough research revealed that there was no such thing as a
typical Australian aborigine, only human beings that fell into many
categories. On Murray River in South Australia, they were described
as extremely hairy of chest and body,[40] which puts them in a class
with western white Europeans, who are probably the world's hairiest
people. In the Victoria Desert they have "copper colored skin,
sloping foreheads, prominent brow-ridges, with almost aquiline
noses, most of them slightly built."[41] In Central Australia they have
"deep-set eyes and broad nostrils. Some of their women-folk . . .
have fair copper tinted hair."[42] On the border between Northern
Territory and Western Australia are "people with Jewish-like pro-
files and prominent noses."[43] Kroeber describes the native Australian as "black-skinned, very broad nosed, long-headed, prog-
nathus, but their hirsuteness, full beards and wavy head-hair take
them out of the pure negroid sphere."[44] Hooten classifies them as a
"composite, predominently white race."[45] Our best conclusion is
that we have here a wide variety of peoples who migrated to the dead
end of the southeast Asian land mass over a period of centuries and
from a number of points of origin. Their mode of transportation
poses no problem: the peoples of the southeast Asiatic archipelagoes
were, from the beginning, competent seafarers with craft far more
seaworthy than the western Europeans used for their first journeys
of exploration. Competent native navigators could have spanned
the Torres Strait between the Malay archipelago and the Australian

39. *Anthropology* (New York: Harcourt, Brace and World, 1948), p. 138.

40. Ronald L. Berndt and Catherine H. Berndt, *The First Australians* (New York:
Philosophical Library, 1954), p. 26.

41. Ibid.

42. Ibid.

43. Ibid.

44. *Anthropology*, p. 148.

45. Quoted in *Anthropology*, p. 158.

mainland, a distance of not more than one hundred miles, in less than a good sailing day.

While they had nothing but wooden or crude stone tools, which classifies them as paleolithic, they did have a highly developed societal system with strict kinship patterns. Kroeber describes the Australians' "social, conceptual and ritual world . . . as definitely elaborate: full of distinct features and precise rules, well interrelated. In fact, nowhere else have theoretical ethnologists and sociologists been able to demonstrate so neat a functional integration of the parts of culture to the whole as among the Australians."[46]

The tribes of Australia, like all primitive societies, possess the ancient concept of the God of Heaven. Early investigators, unable to discover this because of the natives' reluctance to reveal their tribal lore, concluded the Australians were no more than animists without a definite animistic cult. Lang wrote in the *Encyclopedia of Religion and Ethics* that "the idea of a supreme being is not of late appearance in culture, and is not a reflection from human kings. It is found among the democratic tribes of Australia, who, at most, have a 'head man' of the community, while the council of the mature men makes his position more or less constitutional. 'The All Father' is not the glorified ghost of such an one, because He had before death, in the myths, entered the world; and he still exists, usually in a world of His own, above the sky."

Mircea Eliade writes that Kurnai youths are dedicated at puberty rites to the sky-god. "The instructors raise the novices into the air several times, the novices stretching their arms as far as possible toward the sky."[47] He identifies their sky-god as *Daramulen.* Another scholar adds that "it is among the Kurnai, whom on other grounds we have regarded as the most archaic of the tribes, that we meet with a monotheistic belief in its simplest forms."[48]

Another Australian name for the Most High is *Kela di.*

Among the Kaitish and surrounding tribes the name of God is *Atnatu.* In another encyclopedia article, Lang describes the native conception of *Atnatu*: "*Atnatu* was prior to *Alcheringa* or, 'Age of Beginning of All Things'; He arose up in the sky in the very far back past. . . . He made Himself and gave Himself a name . . . he expelled from His heaven a number of His sons who neglected his sacred service, and they came down to earth, to which *Atnatu* sent everything that the black fellow has." It seems highly probable that *Atnatu*

46. Ibid., p. 763.

47. *Birth and Rebirth* (New York: Harper, 1958), p.7.

48. William J. Sollas, *Ancient Hunters and Their Modern Representatives* (London: Macmillan, 1924), p. 311.

is cognate with the ancient Sumerian name *Anutu* or *Anuti*. The same must also be the case with names used by other tribes of the Malay archipelago and the adjacent mainland: for instance, the Radé in Annam use *Anete*; the Laté of Papua use *Anotu*; the Ragetta of New Guinea use *Anuti*; the Katé Tribe of Finschaven in Papua use *Anutule*; the Yabin of Huon Gulf in Eastern New Guinea use *Anoto*; and the Ilcano of Northern Luzon use *Anito*.

Oceania. The island masses of Southeast Asia and the South Pacific furnish one of the most thickly populated and, at the same time, remote areas for the study of our subject.

Streams of migrants left the mainland of Asia for the larger islands, and then the larger islands for the smaller ones and the atolls, in response to the pressure from population. Continued migrations from the interior of Asia caused a blending of racial stocks and languages, resulting in new cultures and ways of life. Scarcely a single atoll more than a few acres large failed to be settled by families and tribes seeking new homes.

This migration could have started as early as 2000 B.C. and continued until the eighteenth century. It consisted of tribes that probably lost their literacy within a few generations after leaving the mainland. The most remote of the islands, Easter Island—a mere 2,030 miles from the South American coast—had a literacy the remnants of which have been discovered within the past century. It seems to be indigenous, although some have tried to identify it with the Indus Valley Script, which has never been deciphered; there are similarities, but both are pictographic so the similarities could be pure coincidence.

The culture of the South Pacific, like most cultures, had two levels of religious concepts. The first European observers saw only the lower level—the superstitions, omens, mana, tabus, the sorcerers practicing contagious and imitative magic, idols, temples, and other paraphernalia associated with religious rites. A prominent ritual was the recital of a lengthy genealogy that ended only when the reciter reached the god from whom his family supposedly descended.

When later investigators entered the field and gained the people's confidence, they discovered that throughout the entire South Pacific the same pantheon was recognized, and it equaled the high-gods of the anthropologists and the Supreme Being of the theologians. Three divine names dominate the scene: *Tané, Tangaroa,* and *Atua*; their attributes are identical and may well refer to the same Being.

Atua is used most frequently by Bible translators. Variations in the spelling by the translators are probably due to the acuity of the hearing of the scribe. *Atua* becomes *Otua* on Tonga, *Aitu* in Rotoma,

Toa in Samoa, *Atu Motua* on Mangareva, and *Akua* in Hawaii where /t/ becomes /k/. *Atea* is universally the God of Space.

Tane is the Creator God throughout Polynesia; *Tane Mahuta* is the Maori sky-god who separated light from darkness; *Tane* becomes *Kane* on Hawaii.

Tangaroa appears as the Creator, self-begotten. In Tahiti he becomes *Ta'aroa*; in Banks Island, *Tagaro*; in Samoa, *Tagaloa-lag*, *Tagaloa* of the heavens; on Easter Island, *Hangaroa* (the God of Oceans), /t/ becoming /h/.

The Americas. The diffusion of the name of God in the American continents is a challenging subject to study; it is also a point of controversy between those who insist that there is no language connection between America and the Old World and those who insist there is.

The fact that each of the language families of the Western Hemisphere contains the universal morpheme for the name of Deity, with allowable variations, suggests separate migrations from several Old-World points of origin. The degree to which the knowledge of God has receded would be a clue to the time of migration from the old world.

It is reasonably safe to say that the migrations to the Americas, following the hiatus that Kroeber postulates between the old cultures—Folsom, Scotts Bluff, Sandia, etc.—and the coming of the later, precolumbian tribes,[49] may have begun as early as 2000 B.C. and continued well into the Christian era.

We are saying, in effect, that the tribes occupying the Western Hemisphere at the coming of the Europeans were not descendants of the hypothetical migrants who supposedly crossed a land bridge some 20,000 to 30,000 years ago. That there was a land bridge we do not question. That it was this old is unsupported by the evidence; this will be examined in another paper.

These older cultures could not have occupied the continents for any long period of time. If an occupation of 10,000 to 30,000 years preceded the precolumbian occupation, the continents would have been virtually covered with the evidences of occupation, including multiplied millions of human fossils. We actually find that all of the artifacts discovered so far would not fill a bushel basket. There are no dwelling sites or hearth sites; sites such as Lindenmeier Cave and Sandia Cave yielded stone artifacts but no evidence of being occupied continuously. There are no human fossils except for footprints associated with dinosaur tracks (which updates the dinosaurs).[50] Wisconsin man (a teen-age female) and Tepexpan

49. *Anthropology*, p. 683.

50. "Footprints in Stone," *Bible Science Newsletter* 10 (April 1972):5.

man (an adult female) have been assigned to this period but their dates are purely conjectural. What is significant is that all of the artifacts of these old cultures have been found in diluvial deposits.

The "half educated and wholly prejudiced Europeans"[51] who explored, traded, and attempted to be missionaries were quite sure that the American natives were less than human and seemed exasperated that such savages should reject European culture and oppose the immigration of these palefaced newcomers. The Europeans totally rejected the culture of the natives, thinking it unworthy of notice. At least 300 years passed before a few Europeans started considering the possible worth of American Indian traits, customs, and beliefs.

The Spaniards ruthlessly destroyed everything in their path and "converted" the natives at the point of the sword. Everything of cultural significance was destroyed as heathenish.

The French Jesuits were quite skeptical when the Hurons in Canada told them that they worshiped the true God of heaven. The missionaries quickly introduced *Bon Dieu* as the proper name of God.

The English colonists' evaluations of the Indians ranged from the "lost tribes of Israel" to cultureless savages unworthy of the graces of the Christian religion. John Eliot of the Massachusetts Bay Colony was somewhat of an exception to the rule. He considered the natives people, preaching the gospel and ministering to them. When he translated the Scriptures into the language of the Mohicans in 1640, however, he assumed that they had no name for God and simply transliterated the English word *God*.

As competent observers started to inquire about the beliefs of native tribes, they discovered that these "savages" were quite mature and reasonable humans whose beliefs and practices ranged from animistic ritual to true theism. They usually had two levels of religious belief and practice: first and most obvious was a ritualism that appeased the ever present malign spirits that surrounded them —spirits of the dead (manism) and natural forces—and which required priests or shamans to administer it; second and not so obvious, especially to untrained observers, a belief in powerful heavenly forces and a high-god who is Creator, Sustainer, and Ruler and who dwells in the heavens. Hartley B. Alexander writes: "There is hardly a tribe that does not possess its belief in what may properly be called a Great Spirit, or Great Mystery, or Master of Life. Such a being is, no doubt, seldom or never concerned anthropomorphically, seldom, if ever, as a formal personality; but if these preconceptions of the white man be avoided, and the Great Spirit be judged by what he

51. "Are Savage Gods Borrowed?" p. 135.

does and the manner in which he is approached, his difference from the Supreme Deity of the white man is not so apparent."[52]

The evolutionary writers either persistently ignored or evaded the evidence of the concept of high-gods. If they acknowledged the concept, they insisted it had been implanted by Europeans or, as Tylor argued, missionaries: "The 'Great Spirit' creator and controller of the universe, of whom we read in modern descriptions of the North American Indians, came from teachings of the Jesuits in the seventeenth century; and similar divine beings elsewhere seem as little genuine."[53]

One of the firmest arguments to refute Tylor's statement is that missionaries who translated the Scriptures into the native languages found, in a majority of instances, a native word or name which included either the universal morpheme for Deity or a colloquial term that expressed such attributes of Deity that the missionaries found it a satisfactory name for God.

P'ere Ragenau, one of the most astute Jesuits, wrote of the Hurons: "Though they were barbarians, there remained in their hearts a secret idea of divinity, and of a first principle, the Author of all things, whom they invoked without knowing him."[54] A Pawnee chief, interviewed by P'ere Ragenau on his journey of exploration and missionary effort through the Mississippi Valley, said: "The white man speaks of a Heavenly Father; we say *Tirawa Atius,* the Father Above, but we do not think of *Tirawa* as a person. We think of *Tirawa* as in everything, as the power which has arranged and thrown down from above everything that man needs. What the power above, *Tirawa Atius,* is like, no one knows. No one has been there."[55] One could fill endless pages with quotations from research reports on the beliefs of tribes from the Aleutians to Patagonia. It will suffice, however, to list representative uses of the universal morpheme in the names of God among the various language families.

The Yuki of Northern California, whose language belongs to the Yukian language family,[56] honor *Tai komol* as the God of Heaven. Neighboring Athapascan tribes, the Huchnom and Kato, use the same term; they probably borrowed it from the Yuki. Other Athapascan tribes in Northern California, the Hupa and Chilula,

52. In *Mythology of All Races,* 10:82.

53. *Anthropology,* p. 218.

54. Hartley Burr Alexander, in *Mythology of All Races,* 10:16, 17.

55. Ibid., 10:80-82.

56. R. F. Heizer and M. A. Whipple, *The California Indians* (Berkeley: University of California, 1965), p. 5.

use a compound name, *Yinantuwingyan*, a term apparently borrowed from their Algonkian neighbors, the Yurok. In Southern California certain tribes of the Yuman language group, a segment of the Hokan-Siouan family, have cognate terms: the Yuma use *Tu Chiapa*, the Juanenos *Tu kma*, and the Havasupai and Hualapai in western Arizona *To chopa*. All of these terms are said to mean "The Benificient One."

Among the northwest coastal tribes we find a variety of forms of the name of the high-god. The Chinook and other tribes of the Salish family from the Columbia River to the Strait of Juan de Fuca have a form of the name that has come to refer to any supernatural power; it also refers to sinister power, particularly among the Chehalis and cousin tribes of the Puget Sound area, and they call it *Timanawas*. James G. Swan writes that the Wilapa Bay Salish tribes believe each man has his own *Tomanowas*.[57] Another term for Deity is *Sahale Tyee*, "The Chief Above." Another Salish form is *Tahoma*, sometimes written *Takkobad* or *Dokibahl*.

In the far north of Canada, the Beaver Tribe uses *Tgha* and other tribes of Athapascana on the McKenzie River use *T'ta Nitosi*. The Tlingits on the coast of Alaska use *Ta hit*. The Nootka on Vancouver Island and their neighbors to the north, the Tsimshians, use *Ti ho*, "The Power of the Shining Heavens." The Haida on the Queen Charlotte Islands use a term equivalent to that of the Tlingits, *Tachet* or *Taxet*. The Kuskowin Eskimos use *Toiten*. The Eskimos on the east coast, Greenland, and Labrador use *Gutip* or *Gudip*, terms that show European influence.

The Siouan tribes of the plains area and their cousins, the Iroquois, use *Wakenda*, sometimes *Orenda*. Many of these people were devout theists.

The Muskoghean tribes—Creek, Seminole, Choctaw—have a concept of God as the Master of Breath, *Esauge Tuh emissee*, which could very well be an onomatopoeic word distinguished by the infix, *Tuh*.

A number of tribes have adopted colloquial terms, either because they had lost the original word or because it had deteriorated and failed any longer to express the dignity of the high-god. Samples are *K'mukamtoh*, "The Old Man," of the Klamath; *Olelbis*, "He Who Sits Above," of the Wintun; *Yuttore*, "That Which Sits on High," of the Babines (Carrier) in Northern British Columbia.

Most anthropologists have a preconceived notion of what they will find as they examine a strange culture. In this way they fail to discover that the native people are really quite human and just as

---

57. *The Northwest Coast* (Fairfield, Wash.: Ye Gallion, 1966), p. 173. Originally published in 1857.

astute as the anthropologist; too often their findings reflect their own thinking rather than that of the informant.

An interesting example is the case of Silas Heck, the last heredi- tary chief of the Chehalis Tribe of the Coast Salish. He had been interviewed by many anthropologists and had become quite cynical. The author knew him as an anthropologist and as a friend. "They would ask questions the way they wanted them answered, so I told them what they wanted to hear," said the old man. He had a vast store of knowledge despite his limited formal education in a frontier school of the 1890s. He was competent in French and English and knew at least four Indian languages well enough to serve as an informant.

His teacher in Indian lore and religious concepts was his maternal grandmother, who was a girl in her teens when Captain Gray en- tered the Columbia River in 1793. The Chehalis Tribe lived inland from Gray's Harbor and had only slight contact with whites before the 1850s. Thus their beliefs were not colored by the teachings of Christian missionaries.

During informal visits I asked the old man about the tribe's con- cept of God and about any lesser gods in which the tribe believed. His answers were frank and uninhibited: "The anthropologists would smile out of the corner of their mouths when I told them we knew and believed in one high-god. They would say that that was just an idea we had picked up from the missionaries. We worshiped God with prayers that I heard my grandmother use when I was a small boy. She never knew any white people."

The colloquial name for the high-god of the Chehalis was *Hawlawk,* meaning "The Greatest Great or Highest High." Some- times they invoked Him as *Sahale Tyee,* the Chinook "Chief Above." He was Creator, Sustainer, and heavenly Ruler. He was pure spirit and could not be pictured. His worship involved no ritual and no priesthood. Shamanism was related only to the *Timanawas* spirits. Silas Heck explained: "There were two groups among our people [the Coast Salish]. There were those who worshiped *Hawlawk* and those who worshiped the black *Timanawas.* The *Timanawas* spirits lived in the forest and were evil spirits, and the spirits of Indians who had died, and came back to haunt. Fourteen-year-old boys would go out in the woods and fast until they got their life vision and totem spirit. They would talk to the *Timanawas* and when they got older they would be medicine men. They would learn from the older medicine men how to make fetishes and beat the drums. We *Hawlawk* people never used drums." Devout theists rejected the ministrations of the medicine men. They had what were called white *Timanawas,* the valuable lore of the tribe that was taught to the youngsters as they grew to manhood: how to use wild foods and herbal remedies, how to stalk deer and snare small game.

Of the lesser gods that appear constantly in the anthropological literature, Silas Heck explained:

> "Sure, we had a long list of totem animals like beaver and thunderbird and eagle and muskrat. We had heroes like the snow brothers and spider woman. These were the people in the stories we told the youngsters around the fire and there were ceremonies in which all of these woods people were acted out. One old story teller could make the story of the snow brothers last all winter, telling a little each night. You white people have the same things: you have Little Red Riding Hood talking to the coyote; you have Mickey Mouse and Woody Woodpecker and stories about knights and dragons. Spider Woman got bad little Indian children and took them away like you have your bogey man. The Hudson Bay people stole our beaver and made it their totem. The English had their totems of the lion and the unicorn. The Americans took our eagle totem."

Unwittingly he separates the levels of religious thought and worship, the sinister from the innocuous, reducing much of the anthropologists' "religious pantheon" to culture heroes.

Latin America. Highly developed cultures such as those of the Valley of Mexico and the Yucatan Peninsula in Central America, Oaxaca and Monte Alban in North America, and the Inca area in South America, demand detailed study that is impossible in a paper of this length. One noteworthy fact is that these cultures seem to have been imported from Asia without the prolonged migrations that produce indigenous cultures. Gladwin, Buck, Heyerdahl, and others insist on the logic of a series of migrations directed by the eastward-flowing equatorial currents to the coast of America between Panama and the tip of Baja California. Such trips from island groups already settled in the South Pacific could have been made in a matter of six weeks or less by these skillful mariners.

Of interest in this paper are the striking correspondences in the form of the name of God. The Aztecs who were conquered by the Spanish had inherited the lore and language of the Toltecs who, in turn, had inherited these from the little known Teotihuanicans. The sequence of these cultures dates back to the time of Christ or before. The term consistently used for God was *Teo,* and the same term was used as a common noun for sacred objects or culture deities. *Teotl* was the tutelary Deity, but *Teo* is used constantly in the language. The ancient sacred city is *Teotihuacan,* "The city of the gods"; *Teocalli* is a temple or sacred place; *Xochipilli cinteotl* is the flower or maize god; *Teoyaoimqi* is the warrior death god; *Teteo innan* is the deity of fertility; *teotlalli* is a wide expanse of land (god land); and *Teoatl* is the ocean or "god water." This is just part of a long list of common nouns and place names in Mexico.

The Aztec-Toltec use of the morpheme /teo/ bears a striking resemblance to its use by the descendants of the Veddoids in India. For instance, *Dulha Deo* is the bridegroom god of the Gonds; *Nagar Deo* is the custodian god of the cattle among the Garwal; *Ghansyam Deo* is the crop god of the Gonds; *Sonal Deo* is the name of the sun god among the Bhils of the Satpura Hills. The *Deo* of the Indians, the *Teo* of the Aztecs, the *Dyu* of Sanskrit-speaking peoples, and the *Deo* of the Latins all correspond.

The pre-Incas of South America, who may have had advanced cultures, used a slightly different form of the morpheme: *Tiahuanaco* is the name of the sacred city; *Titicaca* is the lake on an island which was the home of the gods. The *Tiki* of the Easter Islanders could be in the same line of migration.

The name of the Most High God used by the Amazon drainage tribes suggests another transpacific migration. The Tupi-Guarani use *Tupan;* the Chorotes in the Gran Chaco, *Tumpa;* tribes on the Amazon drainage of British Guiana, *Tuma;* and the Guarani of Paraguay, *Tupa.* These are reminiscent of forms used in the Malay Archipelago: the Loda dialect on Sumatra uses *Toehan;* the Pakkua dialect of Northern Celebese, *Tuhan;* the Makushi of British New Guinea, *Tuma;* and the Battak of Sumatra, *Tuhan.*

The mention of the South Pacific crossings always brings cries of protest from evolutionists, not because of a lack of evidence or logic but because of the violence it does to their "sacred cow," the land bridge of Bering Strait and the 35,000-year period so well established in the textbooks.

The Melanesians and Polynesians were accomplished seafarers probably 1,500 years before the Europeans timorously started to explore the shores of Africa and the poorly equipped and poorly trained Russians sailed along the south side of the Aleutians to seek the wealth of America's north coast. They traveled on seaworthy craft that carried whole families, domestic animals, and equipment. They were adept at fishing and at snaring sea birds. They used celestial navigation. Every island and atoll became settled, obviously by eastward-moving migrations. Is it logical to assume that no parties ever traveled beyond the islands now known to be inhabited from early times? Certainly parties moved eastward in hope of locating new islands and, finding no new islands, would drift or sail on eastward until the inevitable landing on the shores of North or South America.

Conclusions

A study of the universal diffusion of the name and concept of the Most High God, and a comparison of this with the apostle Paul's formula of religious deterioration in Romans 1, leads to several inescapable conclusions.

1. The synthetic scheme of evolution, which begins with animism, magic and fetishism, tabu and totemism, and ancestor worship, advances to tribal gods and divine kings, propitiation of nature and fertility cults, and then reaches the concept of monotheism, is totally without substantiating evidence and contrary to the findings of a number of competent researchers and linguists during the last 150 years.

2. Tribes reached their so-called "primitive savagery" only after they retreated from the worship of the high-god, and their concepts and practices progressively deteriorated.

3. The American continents were populated by mature humans who brought with them the name of the Most High God as the Heaven Dwelling One. They came after the postdiluvian migrations and during the period when the languages of the world were changing from the "one language and speech." And, the original inhabitants of America, Folsom, Sandia, and Scotts Bluff were destroyed by a flood and were not ancestors to the tribes encountered by the Europeans from the eleventh to the sixteenth centuries.

Bibliographical note: sources for the names of God, in addition to those cited in the footnotes, are: Virgilius Ferm, ed., Ancient Religions *(New York: Philosophical Library, 1950); Eric M. North, ed.,* Book of a Thousand Tongues *(New York: Harper, 1938); and Bessie Gordon Redfield, ed.,* A Dictionary of Deities of All Lands *(New York: Putnam, 1931).*

2

The Testimony of Radiocarbon
to the Genesis Flood

Robert L. Whitelaw

Introduction

Since the development of the radiocarbon dating method by Willard F. Libby about 1949,[1] some 20,000 dates have been published in the annual journal *Radiocarbon*. These dates, contributed by over one hundred noted laboratories, represent every imaginable kind of carbon-bearing specimen, both terrestrial and marine, gathered from every part of the globe.

The "Carbon 14 Clock," as it has come to be known, was promoted at the outset as a means of dating events and artifacts within recorded history. It was seen to be a means of dating North American Indian culture and of more ancient cultures of Europe and Asia, timbers from ancient structures, buried tools, sunken ships, etc. At the same time, since the evolutionary origin and time-scale of fossil life was accepted without question, it was fully expected that most "prehistoric" fossils would be far too old to be datable by the carbon 14 clock; the half-life of C-14 is only 5,730 years, and precise measurement using radioactive dating methods is impossible for specimens older than about six half-lives, or about 35,000 years in this case. This would be especially so for marine life buried deep in the ocean floor—supposedly the primeval tomb of earliest life!

Imagine then the surprise in scientific circles (not disclosed in the public literature) to find measurable and valid dates coming in, year after year, covering most of the widely advertised "prehistoric" men and other fossils portrayed to the public as hundreds of thousands of years earlier, and even coal, oil, and natural gas supposedly Carboniferous, all lying within the detectable limits of carbon 14. Even allowing for the possibility of contamination or other errors of

1. Libby's findings were reported in *Radiocarbon Dating* (Chicago: University of Chicago, 1952). A second edition was published in 1955.

measurement, here were dates off by factors of 10 to 100! Famous "cave men" such as Cro-Magnon, Neanderthal, Rhodesia man, Hotu man, Florisbad man, Nebraska man—and even Leakey's *Australopithecus zinjanthropus,* and Howell's Omo Valley findings widely displayed in the prestigious Smithsonian as well over a million years old—all were now found to lie almost within recorded human history.

Among that body of scientists who are unashamed creationists (a not insignificant number) these findings were recognized as just what one would expect who trusts the biblical record. Among scientists who are by no means creationists are some who frankly declare that these findings call for a reevaluation of basic hypotheses. One wrote in 1956 that "as a result of radiocarbon dates, all the previous interpretations of Pleistocene lake history, depth, and position in geologic time must be reassessed."[2] Another frequent reaction is to dismiss the radiocarbon method as unreliable when compared to dendrochronology, varves, etc. Now varves, or ancient lake shorelines, or glacial till, and other such devices can easily be shown to involve assumptions, where prehistoric dating is concerned, that make them far more tenuous than radiocarbon dating. As to dendrochronology, or tree-ring dating, it is admittedly a secondary rather than a primary dating method. For unless a succession of dead and living trees can be found *in one place* with a clear overlap of identifiable ring patterns in each, no complete chronology is possible. Furthermore, the radiocarbon date of a given tree ring is bound to give an age younger than true, since there is a later infusion of younger carbon into that ring from the rising sap of later years—as anyone should have perceived.

As against the above objections, the radiocarbon clock was confirmed by Libby at the beginning by comparison with known archaeological events, and has been increasingly so confirmed year after year. The radiocarbon dates have time and again established dates in Egyptian, Babylonian, and Assyrian history, corresponding well with known synchronisms of ancient and biblical history, and have confirmed the long-suspected fact that the Egyptian dynasties of Manetho were fattened by hundreds of years in various places, with similar errors in Berossus in recording Babylonian history—a typical fault found then and now as vainglorious rulers rewrite history to glorify themselves.

The Carbon 14 Clock Points to Creation

I have shown elsewhere that, from the beginning of the carbon dating method, Dr. Libby was aware of the disconcerting fact that the annual specific production of radiocarbon from solar and cos-

2. *Science* 124 (October 12, 1956):669.

mic radiation in the earth's atmosphere exceeded the specific activity or disintegration rate of the same isotope (C-14) in all living matter by a factor of almost 25 percent. He also recognized the biblical implications of this imbalance: "If one were to imagine the cosmic radiation had been *turned off until* a short while ago . . . the specific radioactivity of living matter would be much less than the rate of production. . . ." (i.e., just as measurement shows). One has only to substitute the word *created* for "turned off until" to perceive that he was looking biblical creation straight in the face! Furthermore, using the two values he measured for specific production and specific activity, I have shown that they point to a creation not longer than 15,000 years ago. Finally, I have shown that the specific production rate before the Genesis Flood could well have been three times greater than at present, which would then mean that, to paraphrase Libby, cosmic radiation was turned off until a mere 7,000 years ago, thus confirming biblical chronology as precisely as one could ask![3]

Early Evidence for the Genesis Flood

Long before anyone knew of the carbon 14 clock and up until Darwin's day, the scientific world recognized the abundant evidence of a worldwide watery catastrophe such as the Genesis Flood. Byron C. Nelson drew attention to this fact in 1931 with this thought-provoking statement:

> What is called "modern" geology has eclipsed Flood geology because of a dislike for those supernatural elements which are the backbone of Christianity. The Flood theory of geology has not been abandoned because it does not satisfy actual geological conditions. There is nothing known about the earth's geological state today which makes the Deluge theory any less satisfactory an explanation of the fossiliferous strata than in the days when the leading scholars of the world accepted it. Rather the contrary—there are facts known now about the geological conditions of the earth remarkably supporting the Flood theory which Williams, Catcott, Harris and others never dreamed of. It is a disregard for God and the sacred record of his acts, and nothing else, which has caused the discard of the Flood theory to take place.[4]

Since Darwin and Lyell, the earth sciences have compiled a mountain of further evidence for the Flood, as Nelson indicates; and

3. "Radiocarbon Confirms Biblical Creation," *Creation Research Society Quarterly* 5 (September 1968): 78; "Radiocarbon and Potassium-Argon Dating in the Light of New Discoveries in Cosmic Rays," *Creation Research Annual* (1969), p. 71; "Time, Life and History in the Light of 15,000 Radiocarbon Dates," *Creation Research Annual* (1970), p. 56.

4. *The Deluge Story in Stone* (Minneapolis: Augsburg, 1931).

before capping this evidence with the dramatic results of radio-carbon dating, it is worthwhile to summarize it:

1. The unquestionable testimony of Scripture: Genesis 6-9, Matthew 24, Luke 17, II Peter 3.

2. Universal flood legends, clearly originating in a great historical event.

3. The convergence of all ancient civilizations and records to an origin about 3000 B.C.

4. Vast animal graveyards and fossiliferous rubble rifts found worldwide.

5. Evidence of a great, sudden, and recent watery cataclysm, followed by a deep freeze, across the entire great north, accompanied by titanic hydraulic forces and crustal upheavals, burying a host of mammoths, mastodons, elephants, and other great beasts in a region now almost devoid of any vegetation.

6. Vast numbers of fossil trees and plants, standing erect, oblique and even inverted while piercing through successive beds of water-laid stone.

7. Abundant evidence of profuse vegetation and a temperate, even subtropical climate prevailing in Antarctica and the northern polar regions.

8. Fossils of all kinds, including almost every modern form of life, all found in sedimentary strata, often at great depth and under great pressure.

9. Inland seashore, unmistakable from the air, as of a world ocean slowly receding, and marine fossils found buried and exposed at every altitude.

10. Vast and numerous rifts, fissures, and lava beds scarring the world ocean floor, all clearly recent and bespeaking some gigantic submarine upheaval of the earth's crust and of thousands of submarine volcanoes in simultaneous eruption as "fountains of the great deep."

And there is much more evidence that is equally compelling.[5]

To this impressive body of qualitative evidence for the biblical flood, the radiocarbon dating method now brings us two independent groups of dates giving quantitative testimony both to the biblical date and biblical extent of the Flood.

Radiocarbon Dates of Terrestrial Specimens Support the Genesis Flood

Out of some 15,000 radiocarbon dates accumulated and published up to 1970, I have shown elsewhere that about 9,670 repre-

5. See George McCready Price, *The Modern Flood Theory of Geology* (Old Tappan, N.J.: Revell, 1935); Alfred M. Rehwinkel, *The Flood* (St. Louis: Concordia, 1951); Henry Morris and John C. Whitcomb, *The Genesis Flood* (Nutley, N.J.: Presbyterian and Reformed, 1961); Immanuel Velikovsky, *Earth in Upheaval* (New York: Dell, 1955).

sented specimens of terrestrial flora and fauna and human cultural deposits. They also included a host of fossils previously thought to be Pleistocene and earlier, some of which I tabulated. I separated these 9,670 dates into three major groups and sorted them into 500-year intervals—after correcting for the obvious error between specific production rate and disintegration rate reported by Libby in 1952. The correction in each case reduces a given date to a younger value.[6]

The objective of the 500-year sorting was to discover any statistical evidence of a period in history during which a sudden increase in deaths was followed by a marked decrease in terrestrial life. The argument was that, if at some point in history a great watery catastrophe wiped out all terrestrial life, a sufficient accumulation of radiocarbon dates from all over the world should be able to demonstrate such a fact by showing a period when all such life essentially vanished, followed by a subsequent build-up to modern times. Likewise, if no such catastrophe ever occurred, a uniform build-up or distribution of terrestrial dates throughout history should serve to dismiss the biblical record once and for all!

With this object in mind, the three groupings used for the 9,670 dates were as follows:

1. Dates associated with men or animals in the Afro-Eurasian land mass.

2. Dates associated with men or animals in the Western Hemisphere.

3. Trees or fossil trees, wherever found, except those felled for tools or structures, or in the form of human firewood or charcoal.

When the dates in these three groups were corrected and sorted as described, the distribution in table 1 and figure 1 appeared. Despite the limited quantity of statistical data, one could scarcely ask for more graphic evidence that some great catastrophe drastically reduced all flora, fauna, and mankind simultaneously in both hemispheres, about 3000 B.C. Could it be mere coincidence that this is the very date of the Genesis Flood, derived by biblical chronology?

Further investigation of the details of the dates in table 1 disclosed no less than eleven points of support for the biblical record:

1. Nature had a recent beginning.

2. In fact nature began about 7,000 years ago.

3. All forms of living matter, ancient and modern, appeared at the same time, as is also attested by the fossil record and admitted by evolutionists.

4. Animals appeared everywhere in quantity, but the human race began with a few.

6. "Time, Life and History." The method of correction is given in the article.

Table 1

DISTRIBUTION OF RADIOCARBON DATES

Number of years before present	Number of radiocarbon dates		
	Man/animals in Afro-Eurasia	Man/animals in Western Hemisphere	Tree deaths only
0- 500	276	496*	154
500-1,000	384	803*	150
1,000-1,500	361	540*	119
1,500-2,000	357	391	108
2,000-2,500	363	253	110
2,500-3,000	344	182	108
3,000-3,500	289	158	102
3,500-4,000	259	114	91
4,000-4,500	198	83	71
4,500-4,950 (Flood)	56	26	35
4,950-5,500	403	249	326
5,500-6,000	185	155	236
6,000-6,500	116	57	119
6,500-7,000 (Creation)	187	43	624
TOTALS	3,768	3,550	2,353

*Dates in these three periods are abnormally numerous because of concentrated research by many universities in American Indian culture.

5. The original world was profuse with vegetation from pole to pole as also attested by the fossil record and admitted by evolutionists.

6. A massive destruction of man, beast, and tree occurred simultaneously on every continent about 5,000 years ago.

7. Specimens predating this event are found largely in sedimentary strata, strongly suggesting that it was a watery catastrophe.

8. After this catastrophe, men and animals repopulated from the Mesopotamian region, reaching the Americas much later.

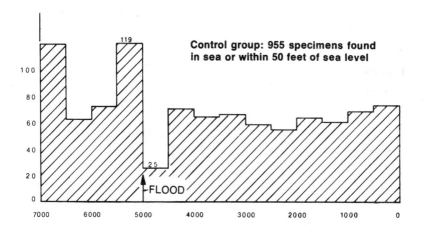

Control group: 955 specimens found in sea or within 50 feet of sea level

119

25

FLOOD

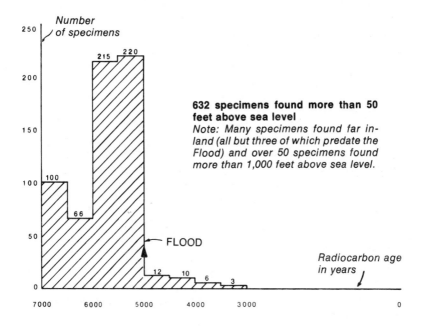

Number of specimens

215 220

632 specimens found more than 50 feet above sea level
Note: Many specimens found far inland (all but three of which predate the Flood) and over 50 specimens found more than 1,000 feet above sea level.

100

66

FLOOD

12 10 6 3

Radiocarbon age in years

Fig. 1 Distribution of radiocarbon dates

9. The same evidence shows that vegetation was rapidly restored but was never again as profuse as before, what with vast deserts and polar wastes such as we see today.

10. The worldwide human population before the catastrophe was large.

11. The biblical chronologies of Babylon, Egypt, and Israel are accurate.

In sum, radiocarbon completely supports the Bible concerning Creation and the Flood in particular and history in general.

Radiocarbon Dates of Marine Specimens Support the Genesis Flood

The published radiocarbon dates from 1949 through 1972 included 1,587 specimens of saltwater marine life, many being in the category of fossils. These were specifically excluded from the terrestrial distribution of figure 1 and therefore represent an independent body of evidence for the Genesis Flood, as we shall see.

The 1,587 marine dates fall into two categories:

1. 632 specimens found in shore cliffs 50 feet or more above sea level or far inland, and gathered from every significant part of the world, including the Great Plains, the Alps, the Andes, and the Rockies. Shellfish predominate (as any fossil hunter or coal miner can testify), but other varieties of marine life are also in this group, including an almost complete blue whale found while excavating for the Ottawa Airport.

2. 955 specimens of dead marine fauna (again mostly shellfish) taken from the ocean bottoms and beaches of the world below high tide. This second group should represent the normal distribution of death-dates in the ocean stretching back to the beginning of time, and should therefore be a "control group" against which any abnormal distribution in the first, land-buried group may be compared.

This selection of 50 feet above sea level as the cutoff between land-buried and sea-buried marine life was based upon figure 2, showing that the annual maximum wave-height off the Grand Banks (one of the stormiest parts of the world) rarely exceeds 50 feet, although once a century this figure may be exceeded.

When the above two groups of dates were corrected for the basic error in the dating system described earlier, and then distributed into 500-year intervals as before, the remarkable pattern shown in figure 3 appears. Of the 632 land-buried marine specimens, all but 31 have death-dates at or before the biblical Flood date, 3000 B.C., and the largest number (220) died in the interval just before the

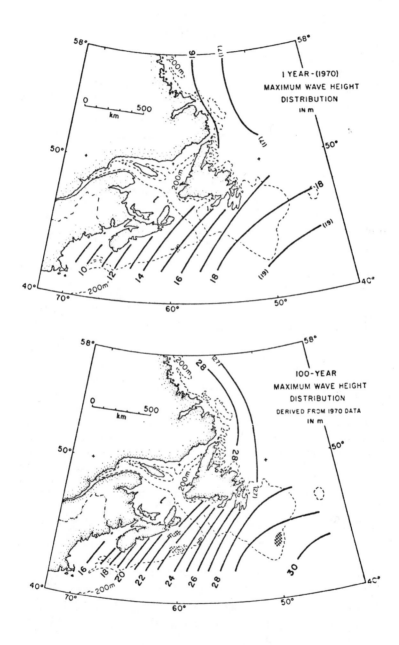

Fig. 2. Maximum wave-height distribution

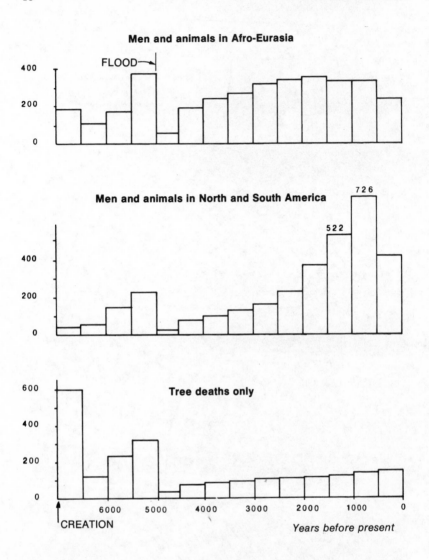

Fig. 3. Radiocarbon age distribution of marine fossils

Flood, resulting in an unmistakable cutoff at about 3000 B.C. as shown. Furthermore, of the 31 possible postflood dates, 10 lie within the probable error of measurement to the Flood, and all but three of the remainder were found on shores within reach of extreme waves such as might be attained once in 100 years.

Looking at the lower half of figure 3, in which the 955 "control group" dates are distributed, we find almost what one would expect from a random sampling of deaths in the world ocean. They are distributed almost uniformly from Creation to the present, except for two anomalies which further tend to support the Scripture record:

1. There is a distinct drop off from 119 to 25 at the Flood date, showing that even in the world ocean, whatever mechanism triggered the uprising of the oceans also must have killed large numbers of marine creatures (exactly what one would expect if the "trigger" were the simultaneous eruption of thousands of submarine volcanoes and upheaval of the ocean floors along the 40,000 miles of undersea crustal rifts).

2. There is a less distinct drop off of dates in the second period after Creation, suggesting an abnormal mortality in the early generations of marine life, which might well be associated with the events of Genesis 3. (Note that a similar drop off in the same period occurs in the terrestrial dates of figure 1.)

In review, then, it is clear that three remarkable facts stand out in figure 3. No matter how one may cavil at the statistical insufficiency of 632 or 955 specimens to cover 7,000 years of marine history:

1. There is a clear disparity between the death-date distribution of marine life found stranded on land (especially those found far inland), and the distribution of dead marine life taken at random from the ocean floor and beaches.

2. All marine life buried on land appears to have died at or before about 3000 B.C., suggesting a massive inundation of every continent associated with titanic forces capable of stripping and redepositing terrestrial sediment and vegetation, mixed with the dead marine life, to the depth of our deepest coal mines, thus accounting for fossils.

3. This cutoff date of about 3000 B.C. for marine life deposited on land, with a simultaneous though smaller cutoff of deaths in the ocean, corresponds exactly with the cutoff date shown earlier in figure 1 for the simultaneous worldwide death of terrestrial life, and both dates correspond exactly with the biblical date and the worldwide extent of the Genesis Flood.

Conclusion

We thus have three bodies of data, painstakingly gathered by science itself, each of which independently attests the accuracy of the biblical record as to both Creation and Flood:

1. An abundance of separate geological and historical "witnesses" to a worldwide crustal upheaval and terrestrial inundation as-

sociated with titanic forces and drastic geographical changes, all in "recent" time.

2. Almost 10,000 terrestrial radiocarbon dates whose distribution *quantitatively* confirms the biblical date and extent of the Genesis Flood, plus some nine other details of biblical history from Creation to the Flood.

3. Over 1,500 radiocarbon dates of marine life whose distribution gives even more dramatic confirmation of the biblical date and extent of the Genesis Flood.

This large, and still-growing mountain of evidence has been gathered by the indefatigable zeal of modern science. Yet that very science, for 150 years, has laughed to scorn the idea of biblical Creation, and has sedulously erased the Genesis Flood from textbooks of geology, archaeology, and paleontology. It would be difficult to imagine a more dramatic example of the truth of Psalm 76:10: "Surely the wrath of man shall praise thee!"

We thus bring into focus the two principal follies of modern science whenever it looks at time, life, and history past: willful refusal to accept the biblical record of Creation and Flood, even when unmistakably confirmed before one's very eyes. We are also instructed in II Peter 3 to expect this very attitude in the name of science when we are "in the last days."

3

Galileo and the Church: Tensions with a Message for Today

T. H. Leith

Introduction

The Copernican revolution began in the first decade of the sixteenth century in an unpublished manuscript entitled *Commentary,* written by a rather obscure household physician in a bishop's palace in northern Europe. Some thirty years later the seeds of its heliocentric reformation of astronomy were to find a stony reception in the minds of two other reformers: Luther called its author a fool[1] and Melanchthon was prodded by it to remark that "wise governments ought to repress the impudence of the intellectuals."[2] In 1543 there appeared in print Copernicus' full defense of his unsettling scheme, the *Revolutions of the Heavenly Spheres.* Seventy-three years thereafter the Congregation of the Index in Rome was to find its doctrines of the centrality and immobility of the sun philosophically absurd and formally heretical, its thesis that the Earth exhibited a daily and annual motion incorrect in philosophy and erroneous in theology. Another seventeen years brings us to the condemnation of Galileo, guilty, said the Holy Office, of holding and defending these evidently false and unscriptural beliefs in his *Dialogues on the Two Great World Systems.* This resulted in the banning of his great book and his spending the remaining years of his life in house arrest.

This century and a quarter, as sketched, suggests a rather unfavorable future for the relationship of the church, Protestant or Roman, to the new astronomy. The origins of the evident tensions

---

1. *D. Martin Luthers Werke,* ed. Otto Clemen, 8 vols. (New York: De Gruyter), 1:419. The comment appears in Luther's table talk, where the possibility always exists that a reporter misunderstood Luther or quoted him out of context.

2. *Corpus Reformatorum: Philippi Melanthonis Opera,* ed. Carolus Gottlieb Bretschneider, 38 vols. (Berlin, 1834-60), 4:679. For the context see Werner Elert, *Structure of Lutheranism,* vol. 1, trans. Walter A. Hansen (St. Louis: Concordia, 1962).

and their context in the second half of the sixteenth and the first half of the seventeenth centuries require some examination, for neither the Copernicans nor the churchmen of the time could see any necessity for the conflict. Each was convinced that it recognized clearly the proper means to a reconciliation. It was the failure to achieve their ambitions, the methods each recommended being so different and unpalatable to the other, which resulted in the impasse and left the horizons so clouded. So much would have been evident to anyone observing events that historic day in June of 1633 when Galileo was sentenced before the Congregation of the Holy Office in the convent of Santa Maria Sopra Minerva. With the benefit of nearly three hundred and fifty years of perspective, we cannot, however, avoid assessing that appraisal. Astronomy was to move in directions as unforeseen by either churchman or Copernican as they were recalcitrant to the techniques prescribed by each camp for harmonizing their mutual concerns. Certainly new principles of accommodation have been offered over the long interval, often fostered by developments in other sciences as each has undergone its revolutionary modern changes. About these too we shall make comment.

Sources of Opposition to Copernicanism

The instrumentalist view of astronomy. Our account must begin with some remarks on the traditions within which Copernican astronomy was to appear so revolutionary. One of these, the assumption that the astronomer's task was to employ whatever mathematical devices afforded a convenient description of the observed behavior of the heavens and reasonable predictions of future events, without any considerable regard for their correspondence to the actual state of affairs obtaining, was of long standing. It is apparent in the astronomy of the Seleucid period in Mesopotamia, which followed the conquests of Alexander, that when astronomers calculated the positions of the sun, the moon, and the planets at various occasions useful for astrological or calendar purposes, they used techniques which involved in essence the plotting of these bodies as points of light moving across the stars as across a graph paper. Nowhere do we find any indication that their motion in three dimensions was considered, or any suggestion of a guiding model of their movements in space.[3]

Even earlier, at the beginning of the fourth century B.C., the Greek philosopher Plato had developed a model of the universe with which he intended to illustrate the planning and design of the world but which he took to be no more than suggestive of how nature might

3. Otto Neugebauer gives a fine summary of this in *The Exact Sciences in Antiquity,* 2nd ed. (Providence, R.I.: Brown University, 1957).

have achieved whatever order was observable. Beyond such convenient myth he would not go, for he took the senses to be as incapable of revealing the truth about affairs on the Earth as in the skies.[4] Examining his scheme and developing one of its ideas, a younger contemporary, Eudoxus, described the motions of each heavenly body as the resultant of clever combinations of eternal and uniform movements in circles centered upon the Earth.

In the next few decades Callippus offered further refinements. Though these schemes introduce three dimensional geometrical models into astronomy, something missing in Seleucid studies, the models are akin to these studies in spirit; apparently no attempt was made to argue that the set of interconnected circular motions combining to move any given planet or the sun or the moon were real, nor was any explanation sought as to why each member of a set should have the particular angular velocity, sense, and axis of rotation suited to it. The models remained no more than useful fictions convenient in aiding our imagination as we predict the paths of the heavenly bodies across the stars.

Of course it was a remarkable feat to show that the complex motions of the heavens were apparently resolvable into components all of which are alike in being uniform, circular, and concentric. If the fit were inexact, all that was necessary was to adjust the relative tilts of the imaginary axes of rotation, to revise the rates of rotation properly, or perhaps to add a further circular motion to the set. The ideal of explaining all heavenly motions as the result of uniform circular motions around the Earth could be maintained to indefinite precision. However, the technique was intended only to predict properly the paths, speeds, and directions of the heavenly bodies against the starry background. It could predict neither the changing size of the moon as it appears to a careful observer nor the great variations in brightness so noticeable on observing the planets. All require a scheme providing for changing the distances of these bodies from the Earth.

That need was fulfilled in the epicyclic astronomy introduced by Heracleides of Pontus in the time of Callippus and developed further by Apollonius in Alexandria during the second half of the third century B.C., by Hipparchus at Rhodes a century later, and by Ptolemy again at Alexandria in the second century A.D. Like the geocentric models, the movements of the heavenly bodies were interpreted as the product of combinations of uniform and endless circular motions, except that here each body would be taken to move on a circle whose center itself moved at a different angular rate on another circle of different size, the center of which in turn might

4. Francis M. Cornford, *Plato's Cosmology* (New York: Humanities, n.d.).

itself be circling the Earth. The Earth was now central only to the imagined shell of the stars.[5]

As with the geocentric schemes, epicyclic devices were capable of indefinite refinement to fit improved observational data and, as with those schemes, epicyclic astronomy saw itself as inventing its devices merely as convenient predictive fictions. Ptolemy took this to be a necessary evil, informing generations of his followers that the complexities of observed heavenly motion seem to defy the ability of philosophers of nature to fathom them. Their causes and their true nature, therefore, remain matters of speculation and controversy. His assessment of the limits of astronomy was still widely accepted by workers in the field in the days of Copernicus fourteen centuries later and for many years thereafter. It provided a major challenge to Copernican astronomers from their own colleagues.

Aristotelian cosmology. Difficulties for the heliocentric scheme arose also from a source of equal antiquity, the philosophy of Aristotle. His great mind had introduced in the mid-fourth century B.C. a magnificent and systematic natural philosophy which still attracted many as late as the seventeenth century. We cannot attempt to outline it here, but various aspects require some mention.

Aristotle employed the devices of Eudoxus and Callippus to interpret the apparent motions of the stars, the sun, the moon, and the planets, with one major revision: these motions arise from the combined effect of physically real but invisible shells moving endlessly at their own angular rates and directions about the Earth. Connected ultimately to the starry sphere revolving rapidly around us once each day, the shells carrying these bodies therefore exhibited both the effects of that daily revolution and the influence of the four or five shells which gave to each its particular drifting path across the stars. From the moon outward, our cosmos became a vast mechanism eternally carrying the heavenly bodies in their cycles about the Earth.

All of this Aristotle saw as quite rational. Only a spherical world could revolve in its own space and exhibit simple symmetry: the former was necessitated by what he took to be the impossibility of a void, and the latter by the requirement that the influence of stellar motion must bear equally upon the bodies within the starry sphere in all directions. Only a finite universe could revolve within the finite period of twenty-four hours, infinite speeds being impossible. Only a mechanism involving a nest of transparent shells could move the heavenly bodies, give them their cyclic sidereal periods, and explain

5. Surveys of geocentric and epicyclic astronomy are available in John L. Dreyer, *A History of Astronomy from Thales to Kepler* (Magnolia, Mass.: Peter Smith, n.d.); and Samuel Sambursky, *The Physical World of the Greeks* (New York: Humanities, 1960).

both how these periods decreased as the bodies lay at greater distances from the starry shell, itself moved by the Unmoved Mover, and the source of motion elsewhere in the heavens.

The centrality of the Earth seemed equally necessary. Beneath the moon, the natural motions of the elements were quite different from the eternal movements of the heavenly and transparent ether. They were linear and had a beginning and end: earth and water naturally move toward the center of the cosmos while air and fire naturally rise toward the shell carrying the moon. The natural place of earth is as close to the center as possible and above it should lie the successive shells of water, air, and fire. Observation appeared to confirm this except that various forces prevent the separation being perfect: Aristotle knew the Earth to be spherical and it did seem to be equidistant from the stars in all directions, water and air do lie successively above it, and the presence of fire was indicated when extraneous matter entered its realm and burned as in the case of the aurorae, meteors, and comets.

To Aristotle the motion of the Earth seemed quite irrational. Were it to be translated through the sublunar region, some force in contact with it would be necessary, and he could find no basis for accepting its presence. Were it to rotate, an equally gratuitous force would be required for rotational motion is not natural to it, and Aristotle's physics of motion required that all movement in any event be caused by some internal or external force. Even a falling stone is moved by its potential to become more earthlike being actualized as it passes toward its natural place in the scheme of things. Clearly he had no concept of inertial movement, gravity, or angular momentum.

His arguments on these and other matters appeared to be so coherent, and his premises seemed so intuitively evident, that his cosmological scheme was destined to find many adherents.[6] At least one weakness, however, is apparent: Aristotle's model of the cosmos cannot explain the apparent variations in distance of the heavenly bodies from the Earth. It was revised to provide for this. In the second century Theon of Smyrna suggested that these bodies be immersed eccentrically within transparent ball bearings, each rolling between concentric shells, a scheme which at once gave physical intelligibility to the epicycles which we have mentioned and carried any body to varied distances from us. A later variant moved the

6. Details in Donald J. Allan, *The Philosophy of Aristotle* (New York: Oxford Univeristy, 1970); L. Edlers, *Aristotle's Cosmology* (Assen, The Netherlands, 1965); Melbourne G. Evans, *The Physical Philosophy of Aristotle* (Albuquerque: University of New Mexico, 1964); Geoffrey E. Lloyd, *Aristotle: The Growth and Structure of His Thought* (New York: Cambridge University, 1968); Friedrich Solmsen, *Aristotle's System of the Physical World* (Ithaca, N.Y.: Cornell University, 1960).

planets themselves along tracks between shells eccentric to the Earth. And, as late as the 1530s, Girolamo Fracastoro, in a book dedicated to the same Pope as Copernicus' *Revolutions* was, introduced a shell of variable density between us and the moon. This he utilized not only to explain the variable brightness of the planets and the apparent changing size of the moon as seen in solar eclipses but to preserve the pristine simplicity of the Aristotelian heavens.

This sort of endeavor might have been of only casual interest to most members of the small astronomical fraternity by the mid-sixteenth century, intent upon their predictive Ptolemaic devices rather than on speculations about the physical nature of heavenly motions, but matters were rather different among certain groups of philosophers and theologians. For these it was more important that Thomas Aquinas in the thirteenth century had brought Aristotelian philosophy and its attendant cosmological system, by various adjustments, into seeming accord with the generally accepted tenets of the Christian faith.[7] Aristotle's teachings therefore played their part in forming a full-orbed Christian philosophy which included both science and theology. If the Copernicans had to provide a serious critique of Aristotelian astronomy and its physical bases, they also had to meet the challenge, flung at them by those who followed Aquinas, of indicating just how the novel heliocentric scheme might be reconciled to the teachings of Scripture in the face of their own synthesis involving a very different system.

Scientific skepticism. A third difficulty facing Copernicus and his followers arises in the context of the relationship between faith and reason. For Aquinas faith had been the necessary approach to biblical teaching while reason provided both the necessary route to understanding those matters on which the Bible was silent and a means to sustaining the credibility of revelation. With reason came a coherent pulling together of our experiences with nature; in this Aristotle was to prove of considerable value. However, Aquinas' analysis was called into question by the debates of the fourteenth century.

One of the seminal minds of that period, Duns Scotus, carried the conclusion that propositions regarding the purposes and nature of God, the immortality of the soul, and similar doctrines were matters of faith to the point that faith became an act of will rather than intellect; we accept revelation because it is prescribed by God and not because it is rational. In turn this implied that the will of God was not constrained by the implication that His decisions must be

7. See Frederick C. Copleston, *Aquinas* (Baltimore: Penguin, 1955).

reasonable. Rather, they are reasonable because they are willed in accordance with His nature.

To William of Ockham that implied further important ideas. If God's will, and nothing else, determines the character of the world among other things, it will then be impossible for us to use reason to lead ourselves back to the nature of God or to His purposes. Reason ceases to support our faith and the goal of uniting philosophy and theology has proven to be a chimera. Further, Ockham believed that only particular things exist and only propositions about these deal with reality. The attributes which one finds in common among the objects and happenings of the world are merely one's concepts and have no claim to reality; they are abstractions and they lie wholly in the mind. The statements, then, which are found in science about these abstractions deal only with names which one has given to them and not with reality directly. The same problem faces the temporal sequence of events which are found in nature. When science discusses the causes of these sequences, which are not directly observed, it is reduced to guessing at the relationships which obtain. Many hypotheses may be offered, none of which can with certainty be said to be true. Our views of the world not only fail to sustain our faith but are thoroughly fallible.

Ockham's teachings were prohibited in certain quarters such as the University of Paris, but at the new universities in Prague, Vienna, Heidelberg, and Cologne they were widely followed and carried influence far beyond their doors. The results were not entirely salutary for the advancement of science. Often there was a loss of interest in careful observation when it was concluded that the hypotheses to be derived were merely speculative. Again, it turned the attention of many to imaginary situations, for example motion in a vacuum, which was taken to be imaginary, revealing only how God might have done things had He wished; or purely abstract studies such as those found at the Universities of Oxford and Paris in kinematics. The latter tendencies were reinforced by the Paris condemnations in 1277 of numerous theses suggesting that God could not have created a world, or indeed a plurality of worlds, different from our own.

Jean Buridan, living in the first half of the fourteenth century, felt the impact of both these condemnations and the teachings of Ockham, his contemporary. His writings reveal the speculative atmosphere occasioned by the former and the continual tentativeness demanded by the latter. For example the question of whether the Earth or the heavens turned daily he left quite open; different theories may always be employed to explain what is observed. Likewise, Nicole Oresme may be found arguing around 1380 that science must remain incapable of deciding upon the motion of the Earth and that only scriptural revelation can settle the matter.

No speculations of the years shortly before Copernicus, though, are as startling as those of Nicolas of Cusa, a scholar and church official who died within a decade of Copernicus' birth. In a work dealing with the limits of human knowledge and in a later note, Nicolas points out a variety of difficulties in conceiving the world in traditional and supposedly rational terms. There was the impossibility of understanding the conception of a finite and bounded spherical universe. Given the realization that the universe must be taken to be indeterminate in size, he asked what sense there was then in talking about the Earth as if it lay in the middle. Again, he suggested that when motion is perceived, it requires that some reference be treated as if it were at rest; but no reference can be chosen, except arbitrarily as tradition had done because we inhabit the Earth, as being absolutely at rest. Thus he concluded that both the heavens and the Earth were in motion in some manner which gave the appearance of a single revolution of the stars counterclockwise about the Earth's axis of rotation, as we look north, every day.

In the end Nicolas was to conclude that even the world view of every thinker is determined by his place in time and space. Because none of these is privileged, he reasoned that it was completely impossible to arrive at a true picture of our world. On that thoroughly skeptical note, epitomizing the extremest form of Ockhamism, he culminates the tentativist trend of numerous thinkers in the pre-Copernican world. It was this sort of attitude which Copernicus had to face, for he was equally convinced of the truth of his ideas.[8]

The Development of Copernicanism

Copernicus (1473-1543). Copenicus' vindication of his system took two tacks, a critique of earlier views defending a stationary Earth and a presentation of alternative arguments for the mobility of our planet. Each was, in turn, a combination of kinematic and dynamic reasoning. The former resting upon a simple description of observed motions in the heavens and the latter upon theories as to the nature of motion.

In treating his geostatic competitors kinematically, Copernicus argued that what we observe of the motions of the stars and the bodies which wander across them may be described equally well by means of his heliocentric scheme. Indeed it did rather better, for

8. The medieval period is surveyed in Alistair C. Crombie, *Augustine to Galileo* (London: Heinemann, 1957); and Gordon A. Leff, *Medieval Thought* (New York: Humanities, 1959).

Copernicus was able to employ contemporary observations to correct varied errors in Ptolemy's predictions and to make improved forecasts in refining the geometry of his own scheme. That was, however, no more than a historical accident, for presumably the Ptolemaic system could be revised in order to account for the newer information. Thus we can explain how Reinhold, in deriving his *Prussian Tables* of 1551, could utilize Copernicus' data and applaud his technical abilities while retaining the essentials of the geocentric method in his calculations. At best, then, Copernicus' argument here served merely to undermine confidence in the Ptolemaic prejudice by offering an alternative; at worst, it left the debate at the skeptical level of Nicolas of Cusa.

The dynamic arguments in favor of a geostatic position were met in an even less satisfying manner. The critique tended to take the form of esthetic judgments or to resort to suggestions for a physics rather different from Aristotle's. The first, unfortunately, reduces the mobility or stability of the Earth to a matter of taste. The second introduced various quite speculative ideas such as the assumption that the rotation of the Earth was natural and unforced and the argument that heavy objects fall toward the center of the Earth because of a natural affinity rather than because the Earth lies at the middle of the universe. The whole was rather poorly thought out and would certainly carry little conviction by the time of Newton. Apparently Copernicus, convinced as he was on other grounds of the correctness of his system, was aware that this required that the old dynamic dogmas be in error. Unable to foresee the new physics suited to his own scheme, he could do no more than make rather gratuitous and fragmentary suggestions as to its nature.

On what basis did he found his convictions? It was the interdependence and coherent simplicity which his model gave to the available observational data. In the Ptolemaic scheme motions on the deferents of the inferior planets and motions on the epicycles of the superior planets took place in a period of one year. The Copernican scheme replaced these by the single annual revolution of the Earth about the sun. Now the relative size of the deferent and the epicycle for any planet in the Ptolemaic scheme could be fixed by observation. Placing this fact beside his replacement just mentioned, Copernicus was enabled to fix the relative sizes of the epicycles of the inferior planets and the deferents of Mars, Jupiter, and Saturn by employing the circles which represent the movement of the Earth at the same scale when dealing with each planet. The result, of course, is that once these relative sizes were known, they became the average orbits of these planets and the order of the planets was established properly about the sun. After several thousand years of debate about the ordering of the planets and about their relative distances, an insight into what a single circle apparently meant in the separate planetary devices used by Ptolemy seemed to resolve the problem in one short step! Where tradition left these matters on a speculative, arbitrary, and erroneous level, the Copernican system pulled them so tightly together that to change any part was to make the whole unintelligible.[9]

Certainly the Copernican scheme now begins to sound worthy of belief. Belief, however, is often a complex psychological matter and thus a function of an idea's agreement with familiar concepts and theories. Many were too astounded by the relative emptiness of Copernicus' universe, by the immensity which it required to explain the lack of observed stellar parallax (it was first found in the fourth decade of the nineteeth century), and by Copernicus' disdain for the logic of the two-level cosmos of the past, to find the new scheme credible. And, of course, biblical scholars could point out its apparent incoherence with the traditional understanding of passages such as Psalms 93:1; 104:5; 75:3; 119:90; 19:4-6; Joshua 10:12-14; Ecclesiastes 1:4, 5; Job 26:7; and II Kings 20:9-11; and the theologian could ask how man's important role in creation was to be reconciled with his position on a mere planet rather than at the center of creation. Clearly an acceptance of Copernicus' understanding would not be widespread in the short term.

Tycho Brahe (1546-1601). In its ability to predict the motions of the heavenly bodies, the Copernican scheme was flawed by the fact that the data which it employed was only a very partial improvement upon that available to Ptolemy. Consequently, tables such as those of Reinhold contained serious errors and modern observations made with accuracy and over a long term were required if the deficiency was to be corrected. It is on Tycho Brahe, the diligent and eccentric Danish astronomer, that the task fell, although his motivation was scarcely to strengthen the Copernican system. Rather, Tycho's ambition was to provide the foundations for a model in which the sun circled a stationary Earth, lying in the center of a spherical cosmos and carrying with it the five known planets. Thereby he hoped both to reconcile astronomy with scriptural teaching as commonly understood and to remove the necessity of placing the stars far beyond the outermost planet as the heliocentric scheme required. His careful observations revealed no measurable stellar parallax, thus either the Earth did not move about the sun in an immense circle or the stellar

9. Further information may be found in Angus Armitage, *The World of Copernicus* (New York: New American Library, n.d.); Thomas S. Kuhn, *The Copernican Revolution* (Cambridge: Harvard University, 1957). See also *Three Copernican Treatises*, ed. Edward Rosen (New York: Octagon, 1971). Two of Copernicus' books have been published in Paris: *Des Revolutions des Orbes Celestes* (1970) and *La Revolution Astronomique* (1961).

regions were at even greater distances than had been thought necessary in Copernicus' day. He preferred the former.

Because his suggested model also retained a nonrotating Earth, it was necessary, as it was in all geocentric systems in which the Earth lacks a daily rotation, to move the planets and sun and moon as well as the stars around the Earth once each day. The individual motions of the bodies moving within the starry heavens, of course, caused these also to drift at various rates across the stars. Tycho was apparently willing to retain this long-standing complexity, in spite of the fact that he took his model to be true to what was actually occurring rather than to be a useful fiction, and in spite of the absence of any physical explanation. However, he did not live to see his data applied in a detailed technical manner to his scheme; his colleague in the short period before his death, Kepler, was to use them to quite different ends. They provided instead the foundation of a Copernican picture of a novel sort, a picture he had intended to avoid.

Tycho contributed, too, we must mention, to the downfall of certain aspects of the Aristotelian world view, something he did intend. His careful studies removed the comets from their traditional place above the atmosphere and beneath the moon and placed them in paths at distances previously reserved for the planets. Aristotle's transparent shells were shattered thereby. Again, his observations of the new star of 1572, because they failed to show any parallax over the eighteen-month period in which it was visible, led him to conclude that it lay in the regions beyond the planets. The supposedly changeless starry heavens exhibited an unforeseen novelty and decay; another facet of the Aristotelian cosmos had been destroyed.[10]

Johann Kepler (1571-1630). Kepler, Tycho's successor as Imperial Mathematician to the Holy Roman Emperor in Prague, obtained Tycho's massive collection of data on stellar positions and the apparent movements of the heavenly bodies. Kepler was already a Copernican, tutored in the system by one of its few astronomical adherents, Maestlin of Tübingen, and the author in 1597 of a small book entitled *The Cosmographic Mystery*, which defended a heliocentric scheme. As is well known, Kepler employed the information to develop a revised Copernican model in which the traditional circles and epicycles of its founder were replaced by elliptical orbits. His conclusions appeared in 1609 in the *New Astronomy*, the same year that Galileo began his equally revolutionary studies with the telescope.[11]

10. See John L. Dreyer, *Tycho Brahe* (New York: Dover, 1963) for details on this.
11. On Kepler's life and work see Max Caspar, *Kepler* (New York: Abelard-Schuman, 1960).

What is less commonly realized is the extent to which Kepler challenged another tradition, the received attitude on biblical teaching regarding the Earth's motion. While he was still a high-school teacher, he had withdrawn a chapter on the subject from his 1597 book to avoid setting off a serious dispute and to insure the approval of the Tübingen faculty, whose approval his printer had required. Later, as Imperial Mathematician he could better afford to treat this contentious question, and he did in the *New Astronomy,* in *Epitome of Copernican Astronomy* (1618), and in the second edition of *Cosmographic Mystery* (1621). Let me quote briefly from the second of these:

> Astronomy discloses the causes of natural phenomena and takes within its purview the investigation of optical illusions. Much loftier subjects are treated by Holy Writ, which employs popular speech in order to be understood. . . . Not even astronomers cultivate astronomy with the intention of altering popular speech. Yet while it remains unchanged, we seek to open the doors of truth. . . . This is all the more reason not to require divinely inspired Scripture to abandon the popular style of speech, weigh its words on the precision balance of natural science, confuse God's simple people with unfamiliar and inappropriate utterances about matters which are beyond the comprehension of those who are to be instructed, and thereby block their access to the far more elevated authentic goal of Scripture.
>
> In our days all the most outstanding philosophers and astronomers agree with Copernicus. . . . Yet the authorities are cast aside by most educated people, whose knowledge is on a level not much higher than the uneducated. Acting by themselves and blinded by ignorance, first they condemn a discordant and unfamiliar doctrine as false. After deciding that it must be completely rejected and destroyed, they then look around for authorities, with whom they protect and arm themselves. On the other hand they would make an exception of these same authorities, sacred and secular alike . . . if they found them aligned on the side of the unconventional doctrine. They show this attitude in connection with the book of Job, chapter 38, when anybody proves by means of it that the earth is flat, stretched to the tautness of a line, and resting on certain foundations, according to the literal meaning.[12]

I quote, too, from the third source:

> Who would deny that God's word is attuned to its subject matter and for that reason to the popular speech of mankind? Hence, every deeply religious man will most carefully refrain from twisting God's word in the most obvious matters so that it denies God's handiwork in nature. When he has understood the most delicately harmonious coordination of the celestial motions, let him ask himself whether

12. The translation is Edward Rosen's and appeared in "Kepler and the Lutheran Attitude Toward Copernicanism," a paper delivered at the Kepler Colloquium, Linz, Austria, 1971.

sufficiently correct and sufficiently productive reasons have been discovered for the agreement between the word of God and the hand of God, or whether there is any advantage in rejecting this agreement and by means of censorship destroying this glorification of the boundless beauty of the divine handiwork. The ignorant refuse to have respect for authority; they rush recklessly into a fight, relying on their numbers and the protection of tradition, which is impervious to the weapons of truth. But after the edge of the ax has been struck against iron, it does not cut wood any longer either. Let this be understood by anyone who is interested.[13]

Two aspects of Kepler's comments deserve special note here. For one, the coherent simplicity of Copernican astronomy and the discovery of a mathematical regularity in nature enunciated in Kepler's famed three laws of planetary motion (the third appeared in 1619 in his *Harmony of the World,* the first two in the *New Astronomy* a decade earlier), together with a welter of speculative musical analogies, astrological theory, and mystical theology had convinced Kepler that he had indeed uncovered in part the true handiwork of Deity. His choice of the most eminent philosophers and astronomers, all Copernicans, was colored by this belief. We assume that he included Galileo, unaware likely of Galileo's distaste for Kepler's approach, but he clearly ignored his Aristotelian and Ockhamist philosophical opponents, those who found the lack of a physical basis for his system disturbing, and astronomers for whom a Tychonic scheme more readily fitted their predilections.

For another, "authority" in matters astronomical was not only handed to Copernican sympathizers but removed from its traditional tenure by biblical exegetes, Aristotle, and those who believed that astronomical work must resort to fictions. His point that tradition was employed only when convenient to current opinion was a worthy one, but most of his contemporaries were unprepared to recognize it; novel ideas, even if founded upon evidence, often have to await a new mind set before they are accepted, and only then are the shortcomings of traditional authorities comprehended.

Galileo (1564-1642). In 1609, the year when Kepler's elliptical orbits were presented to the public, Galileo Galilei was a respected but rather obscure professor in Padua actively seeking, after seventeen years in the post, an improvement in his position. In that summer he first heard of a Dutch device being exhibited there (it was likely modeled upon an Italian instrument of 1590 about which he had been equally uninformed) and in haste experimented until he had discovered its secret. Constructing a telescope of some ten diameters magnification, he proceeded to employ it both for as-

13. Ibid.

tronomical purposes and for personal promotion to the positions of Chief Mathematician at the University of Pisa (though he agreed that this would be without teaching duties and that he would not settle there) and Philosopher to Cosimo Medici, the Duke of Tuscany, in Florence. This move from Padua, under the protection of the independent Venetian state, he was later to regret, for it probably placed him more readily into the hands of the Inquisition.

On receiving a copy of the *Cosmographic Mystery* in 1597, Galileo had informed Kepler that "many years ago I became a convert to the Copernican theory." In 1610 his little book on his telescopic studies, the *Sidereal Message,* first publicly announced his position. It contained evidence of irregularities on the moon, thus denying the traditional perfection of the heavenly bodies; evidence of many previously invisible stars, indicating that the import of the heavens could scarcely rest upon what the naked eye had observed throughout history; evidence of a lack of noticeable stellar magnification, which suggested that the stars were farther away than indicated by past opinion; and evidence of the presence of moons orbiting Jupiter, which discredited the uniqueness of the Earth and strengthened the possibility that it orbited around the sun like the other planets. Later, in 1613, the Academy of the Lynx-eyed in Rome, of which he was a member, published his discoveries at Florence of the phases of Venus, which demonstrated its movement about the sun, and of sunspots, whose existence suggested imperfections on that body and whose paths indicated that it rotated.

None of these, however, was difficult to reconcile with a Tychonic model, as his friends among the Jesuits at once recognized. But Galileo refused to countenance that. Then, between 1613 and 1615, Galileo wrote a series of letters attempting to show that the Bible could be interpreted in a Copernican manner. This evoked speedy reaction because it was his first clear challenge to traditional biblical scholarship. Why did he take this risky step? Partly, it would seem, because of his desire to see the church firmly support the new truths about the world revealed to the careful observer, and partly because of his firm conviction that he was right in calling for a new foundation to the philosophy of nature, one with a Copernican outlook, based upon a proper physic and the quantitative method on which he had been laboring for many years.

Galileo is sometimes seen as a scientist challenging the authority or correctness of Scripture. He did nothing of the kind, for he never questioned the harmony of God's revelation in nature and in the Bible; what he did doubt, like Kepler, was the correctness of certain interpretations of the Bible, expounded when other world views and astronomical attitudes were still plausible, and the propriety in many cases of reading any technical meaning into it at all. What was disconcerting to his opponents was the basic attitude toward the

Bible and the church which lay behind this, for it seemed to imply that biblical teaching was never competent to challenge science and that the church lacked authority in matters of biblical interpretation.

If Galileo pleaded that there could be no conflict between well-founded science and the non-(or pre-) scientific language of Scripture, they could reply that no science was so secure as to be beyond question and that, as a scientist, he was incompetent to judge whether passages long used to defend the immobility of the Earth were, in the Hebrew, technical or not. If Galileo wished to tell the church how to interpret Scripture simply to fit what he took to be a solidly-corroborated scientific doctrine, they could argue that this took ultimate authority from the church and placed it in the hands of an individual, an approach suited to heretical Protestantism and anathema to the position so clearly taken by the Council of Trent.

The Dominicans, of course, saw an additional danger in Galileo's thinking, for they were consistently Aristotelian in their natural philosophy. Galileo had, with his espousal of a new physics and of Copernican doctrine, hurled the gauntlet in their direction. From their perspective Galileo was upsetting the entire world order and in particular he was challenging the real synthesis between the Christian faith and Aristotelian philosophy so firmly established since the time of Thomas Aquinas. To the Jesuit followers of Tycho, Galileo also seemed to be making claims for the truth of Copernican doctrine which were unjustified and to be asking the church, of which they were the defenders, to make major concessions on a flimsy scientific basis.

Before long Galileo was hearing from Rome. In the early months of 1615 Cardinal Barberini, through a friend, cautioned Galileo to treat Copernican ideas as fictions. The head of the Jesuit College, Cardinal Bellarmine, a month later was also offering his opinion. In response to a small book by a Carmelite priest, Foscarini, favoring a reconciliation of biblical interpretation with Copernican ideas, he wrote the author a letter, making three points. The first was that the affirmation of the truth of Copernicanism would irritate theologians and Aristotelians, injure the holy faith, and make Scripture false. Secondly, the church, after the Council of Trent had prohibited biblical exposition which was contrary to the common agreement of the church fathers, could hardly support interpretations of portions of the Bible that were contrary to those of its earlier teachers and all modern scholars; indeed, a denial of what the church believes to be the clear meaning of biblical revelation is heresy. Finally, the church would revise its interpretations only if and when the Copernican theory was proven. Within weeks Galileo saw the letter and within months he was in Rome to do battle.

But as the Tuscan ambassador put it, "this is not the place to come arguing about the Moon, nor in this age, to defend or introduce any novel doctrine." And, as a friend of Galileo had remarked, "if new things are introduced . . . someone amplifies, another alters. . . . Your ideas about the . . . bright and dark areas of the Moon introduce an analogy between that body and the Earth, someone amplifies this to suggest that you are putting people on the Moon, the next person begins to ask how these can be descended from Adam or how they might have come out of Noah's ark." The church had, of course, a convenient way out, for Galileo had as yet offered no demonstration of the Earth's motion not subject to alternative interpretation. Galileo now essayed to provide one: his notorious argument from the tides which appears to violate his own physics and to be quite incorrect.

It is unlikely that even had it been valid it would have had much effect under the circumstances. The theologians, asked by the Holy Office for an opinion on the merit of the heliocentric doctrine, never considered it and thus never considered revising traditional biblical exegesis. Instead, they judged the idea that the sun was central in the universe and immobile to be philosophically absurd and formally heretical. The thesis that the Earth had a daily and annual motion, and that it was not central in the cosmos, they declared to be incorrect in philosophy and erroneous in theology. Within less than three weeks after Galileo's arrival in Rome, the Congregation of the Index prohibited all Copernican writings. The Copernican revolution ended for church officialdom, it seemed, in March of 1616.

The Pope now instructed Cardinal Bellarmine to inform Galileo that the belief that the Earth moves about a stationary and central sun was unscriptural and thus he could not teach, defend, or hold it. A long debate has centered around whether Galileo did, in fact, heed the Cardinal. A purported minute of the meeting indicates that he did, while a letter from Bellarmine to Galileo quite clearly assumes that Galileo had not abjured his opinions. In any event, Galileo appeared to be defeated for he could no longer defend the doctrine which he so firmly believed.

Galileo was publicly silent for several years after the disturbing events of 1616, but his private opinion was likely that which he expressed some time later. "Can anyone question that, when minds given their freedom by God are placed in abject submission to the will of others, serious unrest will follow? When we are instructed to reject our senses and place them under the fancies of others? When total incompetents are permitted to judge experts and handle them as they wish? It is these novelties which may well result in ruining commonwealths and subverting the state." Melanchthon would have been astounded at that final twist! To acquaintances he could be subtly ironic, commenting that he understood how necessary it was to accept the decisions of his superiors, of those led by a higher knowledge than his poor mind could achieve, and then asking them to read his works as poetry or a dream because "I esteem somewhat this vanity of mine."

In 1623 the Academy of the Lynx-eyed published a brilliant essay on scientific method, entitled *The Assayer* and dedicated to Urban VIII, the former Cardinal Barberini.[14] Hearing of Urban's favorable response, Galileo traveled to Rome the following spring to see if he could obtain from the Pope greater freedom to discuss his Copernican thesis. He was told to go ahead but to treat it only as a useful hypothesis because God need not do things in the way which we imagine. Now 60, Galileo began the preparation of his *Dialogue Concerning the Two Chief World Systems*[15] and completed it early in 1630, some six years later. It came from the press in 1632 and was suppressed soon after an ecclesiastical commission, activated by Galileo's opponents, reported that it was really a defense of Copernican doctrine. Its author was called to Rome and charged with violating the injunction of 1616.

Galileo's defense lay in Bellarmine's letter and the Pope's conversations, allowing him freedom to discuss the doctrine. His opponents brought forward the purported minute indicating that he had been restricted more severely. Galileo replied that he could recall no restraint on his discussing Copernican ideas and that the *Dialogue* did not defend these ideas but instead treated them as hypotheses. However, even if his first plea might be successful, the second was hardly credible. After all, the *Dialogue* was clearly intended as a convincing argument for a new world view; it was aimed at converting the intelligent reader from traditional outlooks by reporting the wonders to be learned from nature. As a result he was found suspect of heresy, required to abjure sincerely and to curse and detest what the church considered to be erroneous and unscriptural, and sentenced to house arrest for an unstated term. He was still under this formal imprisonment at his death in 1642.[16]

14. This and other shorter writings by Galileo are in *Discoveries and Opinions of Galileo,* ed. Stillman Drake (New York: Doubleday, 1957). See Edward Rosen's review in *Journal of the History of Ideas* 18 (June 1957): 439-48.

15. *Dialogue Concerning the Two Chief World Systems,* trans. Stillman Drake, rev. ed. (Berkeley: University of California, 1967); or *Dialogue on the Great World Systems,* ed. Giorgio De Santillana, rev. ed. (Chicago: University of Chicago, 1953).

16. Galileo's methods, life, and trial are discussed in: Ludovico Geymonat, *Galileo Galilei* (New York: McGraw-Hill, 1965); Carlo L. Golino, ed., *Galileo Reappraised* (Berkeley: University of California: 1966); Alexandre Koyre, *La Revolution Astronomique* (Paris, 1961); Giorgio De Santillana, *The Crime of Galileo* (Chicago: University of Chicago, 1955); R. J. Seager, *Galileo Galilei* (New York: Oxford University, 1966); Ernan McMullin, ed., *Galileo: Man of Science* (New York: Basic, 1968); Jerome J. Langford, *Galileo, Science and the Church,* rev. ed. (Ann Arbor: University of Michigan, 1971); Stillman Drake, *Galileo Studies* (Ann Arbor: University of Michigan, 1970); Alexandre Koyre, *Etudes Galileennes* (Paris, 1966); Alexandre Koyre, *Metaphysics and Measurement,* trans. R. E. Maddison (Cambridge: Harvard University, 1968); M. Clavelin, *La Philosophie Naturelle de Galilee* (Paris, 1968).

The Strategies and Impact of the Copernicans

It is worth asking whether the *Dialogue* contained anything really novel in favor of the Copernican scheme. It did, even if we ignore the first printing of his strange tidal theory mentioned earlier. For one thing it mentions the annual variation in the paths of the sunspots, first reported in 1613 by Francisco Sizzi, a rather puerile critic of Galileo's early telescopic work, and indicating that the equator of solar rotation was inclined to the ecliptic plane. The inclination, of course, causes a change in the angle between the sunspot paths and the ecliptic from season to season, in a yearly cycle, and Galileo noted that the obvious reason was our annual motion about the sun. It is true that the apparent paths of the spots could be explained in the Tychonic model also, though the Earth is totally stationary within it, but it would require very complex movements of the sun which Galileo considered quite unlikely.

The other novelty is the *Dialogue's* profound dissimilarity to the great astronomical treatises which had preceded it. Nowhere does Galileo care to explore the details of the revolutions of the planets or of the moon and seldom is it mathematical. Apparently he cared as little for kinematic descriptions like Kepler's, even if it were claimed that they were true, as he did for fictional devices. The latter tended, he thought, to perpetuate the dichotomies of the ancient two-level cosmology while the former continued to bind the physics of motion in its terrestrial fetters. Instead, Galileo's ambition was to emphasize the geodynamic aspects of a Copernican world view and to call for the extension into the heavens of the physics which he was actively building on Earth.

Galileo, of course, recognized the coherence provided by Copernicus in placing the planets about the sun in a specific order, but even this seemed to be merely an esthetic judgment carrying weight only for a mathematician. In its place Galileo wished to offer evidence of the legitimacy of Copernicus' basic insight: evidence of the inability of traditional argument to falsify the motion of the Earth and two new physical proofs of its movement; evidence of the similarity of the planets and the moon to the Earth; and evidence of the similarity of the planetary and lunar motions to those exhibited in terrestrial physics.

The alternative which he aimed to falsify was the Aristotelian philosophy of nature. Ptolemaic astronomy was attacked only indirectly because of its Aristotelian facets; its mathematical devices, or modern improvements upon them, were unimportant to Galileo's concerns. In this excercise he prospered, seriously undermining Aristotelian physics here and later in his *Two New Sciences*.[17] He was

17. *Dialogues Concerning Two New Sciences* (Magnolia, Mass.: Peter Smith, n.d.).

perhaps less successful against Tycho's doctrine. But his arguments unfortunately did little for the kinematic credibility of Copernicanism, for they left the moon and the planets circling the Earth and the sun at constant angular velocities, just as a ball would circle the center of the Earth endlessly if rolling on a frictionless surface. This was much too simplistic after Kepler's labors. If he criticized others for "saving the appearances," he could not even do that much himself.

Galileo wrote in *The Assayer* that the universe stands like an open book, "but we can understand it only if we begin by learning to comprehend its language and interpret its characters [for] it is written in the language of mathematics and its characters are circles, triangles, and other geometrical shapes." But it would seem that his agreement with Kepler, who might have said the same thing, was more apparent than real. It might have been repeated, too, by Galileo's younger contemporary, René Descartes, with even more disparity of meaning. Certainly it was in the spirit of the many Renaissance figures who read in nature innumerable mathematical analogies, often in defense of traditional cosmology, and with whom Galileo could scarcely agree.[18] Even the follower of Ptolemy, arguing that his mathematical devices were capable of being made adequate to prediction and thus should not be matters of contention among astronomers, could have enunciated the same creed. But how varied the implications, how diverse the predispositions, how conflicting the connotations!

Clearly, the meaning of the mathematization of nature in the Renaissance is, if not obscure, complex. It is dangerous simply to label it Platonic or Pythagorean, as is often done, for the adjectives can indicate an *attitude* as well as a *position* or indeed an assortment of modifications of each. Copernicus' position was not that of a Platonist or Pythagorean or he would have agreed that the mathematical patterns of nature must remain hidden from us. Rather, like Tycho and Kepler and Galileo, he believed that nature could be treated in mathematical terms, that we seek out the mathematical relations by observation and experiment, and that our knowledge of nature's structure is gained by intensive study of limited areas of experience. Even the rationalist Descartes would say, "God could well have arranged things in countless ways, the way which He actually chose ... may be determined only by observation." But

18. Of interest here is Constantinos A. Patrides, "The Numerological Approach to Cosmic Order During the English Renaissance," *Isis* 49(December 1958): 391-97. The importance of the number seven seemed more suited to a geocentric cosmos with seven bodies circling it than to a sun orbited by six satellites. Including the central body, on the other hand, could have made the heliocentric view more suitable than its alternative. Numerology is clearly highly selective in its evidence and subject to endless adjustment to fit any predilection.

their methods were different: Copernicus and Kepler were willing to find patterns and to suggest novel (and unsatisfactory) physical foundations for them; Tycho was prone to assume much of Aristotle's physics and traditional biblical exegesis and to work from there; and Galileo and Descartes could overlook details about planetary motions in trying first to move their terrestrial physics into the heavens.

Methodological diversity is an indication of disagreement as to tactics and strategy in resolving a scientific problem. It is often an expression, too, of dispositional disaccord, as when we compare Kepler's, Galileo's, and Descartes' philosophies of nature on a broader level than their consonance regarding a mathematical world. Kepler was mystical, sympathetic with aspects of astrology, and convinced that the cosmos was finite; Galileo was hardheaded, opposed to the occult to the point that he denied the moon's influence on the tides, and of mechanistic and materialistic bent; and Descartes could offer sincerely many certitudes about the world assumedly based only upon reason, reduce matter to space, and found his physics upon the direct activity of God. Their followers, in addition, could disagree vigorously about the implications of these and like matters.

So could those seeking a reconciliation of their views with theology. Kepler's astrology would be suspect and, in time, his finite world would be interpreted as discrediting the power and glory of God. Galileo's comment in *The Assayer* that "I don't believe that anything more is necessary to give rise to our tastes, smells, and sounds than that external objects have sizes, shapes,numbers and less or greater speeds" was destined to stir endless controversies about materialism and mechanistic philosophy. Recall, for example, what affinities one can find between these in Newton's apologetics and then remember Leibniz's opprobrium.[19] And Descartes was condemned widely because his physics was difficult to reconcile with transubstantiation, while Jansenists and Calvinists, on the other hand, favored its determinism.

It is critical, then, that we realize that the implications of the Copernican revolution for the church lay not only in its simple challenge to traditional exegesis of a few passages or even to the central place, geometrically if we will, of man and the drama of the fall and redemption. Those may have been clearest at first, as they were to Melanchthon or to Osiander, who wrote the notoriously misleading preface to Copernicus' *Revolutions,* but it required the social upheavals and tensions of most of a century to get Rome to

19. See *Leibniz-Clarke Correspondence,* ed. H. G. Alexander (Manchester, England, 1965); and Frederick C. Copleston, *A History of Philosophy,* 8 vols. (New York: Doubleday, 1946-67), vols. 4-6.

follow Melanchthon's advice and to repress what he had called the impudence of its Copernican intellectuals. Even then it required peninsular and Vatican politics of which we have given no account here, and an apparent frontal attack upon vested authority, to bring it into action. The church moved when goaded and when it recognized just who Galileo was making the final arbiter on hermeneutical rules whenever science was involved, and when they saw that this implied giving to a novel astronomy and physics the power to break down the harmonious world of tradition.[20]

How little, though, the church, or a Galileo for that matter, could see the many other consequences of the revolution, for it continues to our day. By complex and intertwining paths it led to Newton's and Laplace's physics and on to Einstein, to deism and then agnosticism, to new cosmologies, to Descartes and Locke and on through Hume and Kant and Spinoza to contemporary philosophy, and to a thorough revision of man's view of himself exhibited by a modern theological conservative as well as by a Marxist or a Bertrand Russell.[21] We are, of course, not arguing that a Copernican system was the sole or even a conscious source of these developments; we are saying that the scheme, its developing physical base, and the philosophies in which these were initially applied, carried diverse and startling implications. No suppressions of the next centuries after Galileo could contain them; an increasingly pluralistic society or complex of societies never can.

This is the case with all novel scientific ideas. They cannot be restrained if the human mind is to be permitted a measure of curiosity and if its suggestions about the world are to be put to test. The contemporary church, as a society, is surely obliged to accept this just as it must if its conception of a natural revelation of God is to be taken seriously. But the thinkers who enunciate ideas in their initial or developing forms, or who employ them, do so within varied philosophical attitudes and as well use the ideas in constructing at

20. The church conveniently ignored the degree to which its own cosmology had accepted much of Aristotle and many observational evidences which eliminated things like the flat earth, the tabernacle-shaped world, and the sublunar firmanent of earlier traditions.

21. See first Vern L. Bullough, *The Scientific Revolution* (New York: Holt, Rinehart & Winston, 1970); A. M. Duncan, *The Scientific Revolution of the Seventeenth Century* (Bath, England; James Brodie, 1969); Eustace M. Tillyard, *The Elizabethan World Picture* (New York: Random House, n.d.). Then see Marjorie H. Nicolson, *Science and Imagination* (Ithaca, N.Y.: Cornell University, 1956); Marjorie H. Nicolson, *The Breaking of the Circle*, rev. ed. (New York: Columbia University, 1960); Robert H. Kargon, *Atomism in England from Hariot to Newton* (New York: Oxford University, 1966); Victor I. Harris, *All Coherence Gone* (New York: Barnes & Noble, 1966); Hedley H. Rhys, ed., *Seventeenth-Century Science and the Arts* (Princeton, N.J.: Princeton University, 1961); Richard S. Westfall, *Science and Religion in Seventeenth-Century England* (New Haven, Conn.: Shoe String, 1958). All deal only with the beginnings of the process.

least partially novel world views. Dialogue on philosophical issues and a person's private beliefs are even more difficult to constrain, as the prohibitions of the Holy Office on Copernicanism, the Nazis, the Stalin years, and denominational history have reminded us sharply. With that fact, too, the organized church must come to terms in our time.

Perhaps the warning by Galileo should be recalled here: permit tradition and authority in ecclesiastical matters to overrule empirical data and scientific expertise, and one may ruin and subvert an institution. Ideas, observation, and experimentation exist in free places and with free persons, and they eventually erode and invade, discrediting the authority which attempted to proscribe them. The other side of the coin, however, recognized by Melanchthon and the Holy Office,[22] was that scientific discoveries involve questioning and upheaval equally capable of destroying traditions and authority which are now taken to be illegitimate. The church's obligation to foster new insights and to recognize the breadth of revelation should help to preserve it from Galileo's prophecy. How it handles the implications of these, and the philosophies attendant upon them, will govern how satisfactorily it survives the impact foreseen by the Lutheran scholar and Roman officialdom.

What the Church Must Offer Science

Let us look, in conclusion, at the opportunities afforded the church in the light of these considerations, for we should see matters positively. It is no longer sufficient to rest quietly, like the Holy Office in 1633, in the belief that novel scientific ideas seem, at first glance, to be philosophically absurd and/or formally heretical. Too often we have heard that some theory is imperfectly evidenced and that the church need not treat it seriously. It may be so, but when a theory is corroborated extensively by severe testing and gains wide recognition, that attitude is no longer acceptable. Too frequently we react to the unfamiliar as if it were preposterous, though there is often no easy resolution to such a psychology except time. Likewise, too commonly our mind set on matters exegetical or theological causes us to confuse heresy with the unusual or the unfamiliar.

Let us look first at exegesis. Copernicus, Kepler, Thomas Campanella in his *Apologia pro Galileo* (1622),[23] and Galileo all recognized

22. Oddly enough the Spanish Inquisition was less concerned. See Henry Kamen, *Spanish Inquisition* (New York: New American Library, 1965), pp. 101, 102, 293-96. Compare also R. H. Popkin, "Scepticism, Theology, and the Scientific Revolution in the Seventeenth Century," in *Problems in the Philosophy of Science,* eds. I. Lakatos and A. E. Musgrave (Amsterdam, 1968), pp. 1-39.

23. A translation of G. McColley is available in *Smith College Studies in History,* 1936-37. It is criticized in part by Edward Rosen (see n. 14).

that hermeneutics is, more than was admitted, a human art influenced by the world view of the scholar. We must understand this, too, however high is the exegete's scriptural view. If we do, we must expect the biblical scholar to give more serious attention than he often has to the likelihood that many passages are prescientific or nonscientific. The scientist is obliged to inform him of the extent of his anachronisms so that he may be more perceptive. We should fully expect that the process will be attended by theological revisions as well. Perhaps this sounds gratuitous or even supercilious but it is the lesson of church history that the process works, in part, that way. If it is learned, the church may then offer to thinking men considerable a priori flexibility within which new discoveries may be accommodated. No longer need it appear to be in continual and reluctant reaction. Had the church given theological and exegetical room for the scientist and philosopher to move in the past, the ranks of both camps might contain rather more members with respect for biblical authority than they do now.

Of course, it may be remarked that many biblical interpreters and many church bodies permit room for most, if not all, philosophies and interpretations of scientific ideas. Clearly this overly broad accommodation can only be because of a lower view of the authority of Scripture than is warranted by the evidence. It is the consequence of critical studies based upon certain philosophies about science and certain constructions of scientific theories which deny a supernatural view of the world and result in a debased view of inspiration. It is the product not of scientific theories, at least well-founded ones, but of fundamentally humanistic and naturalistic predispositions. Nor is it the necessary consequence of the process espoused above. There we speak of recognizing the intent of Scripture in its own terms and of a biblical theology prepared to deal with matters which scientific evidences soon may well place before us.

It brings us, though, to a second point. Scientific theories, while still highly tentative, are often accepted or rejected by many upon grounds such as prejudices for or against past ideas; one's world view; one's esthetic tastes; or trepidation about, or wishful ambitions for, their moral or philosophical consequences. Indeed, those matters play a part in developing the theories in the first place. These factors are as unavoidable as they are subjective. Certainly the church has no obligation toward such theories except to foster the freedoms necessary to test them out carefully; and, if it firmly believes that natural and special revelation cannot fail to be in harmony, it need expect no irremediable difficulties in synthesis. It does, though, have obligations to determine its stance toward the practical applications of theories operative at any time or likely to be put into effect in the foreseeable future. Biology and biochemistry afford current instances of this necessity. The questions are ones of individual and social morality and on these the church must speak. If it does, coherently and intelligently, it has the opportunity to recover an influence lost by its past failings in this respect.

This brings us to the last opportunity to be mentioned here: the chance to support the development of Christian philosophies of man, the world, and action. The Scriptures and scientific knowledge leave extensive room for speculation about the nature of creation and providence or the meanings of history; for interpreting the arts, literature, or science; and for constructing political, psychological, or social models. We mention these only as examples. In a world filled with philosophies based upon humanistic premises, the church has offered too little in the way of systems built upon theistic and biblical premises, and the systems it has offered have paid inadequate attention to current knowledge and situations. True, the church has seen its philosophers in open disagreement in the past and it has observed disturbing implications being drawn from positions which it thought were sound. Perhaps this is one reason why it has failed to offer the sort of support it should to new ventures and why it has too often satisfied itself with traditional and simplistic treatments of the many matters attracting concern and interest in the society around it and in its own communion. This is an insufficient reason. Men are fallible and their schemes imperfect; tensions must exist when theological emphases and the matters which interest thinkers differ, but problems and opportunities must still be faced. Only one illustration will be offered.

We live in an age in which science and its offspring technology have revised, in a way few foresaw a quarter century ago, the conditions of our lives. It is apparent that our ability to master the forces of nature around us is immense and increasing. It is clear that we have in our hands the awesome power to create, with rapidity and in profusion, new and little-understood social possibilities. But science and technology have also altered the manner in which we look at ourselves, and they have destroyed some of our values while creating others. Here lies their potential for both good and evil, for the process continues.

Yet, in the face of this, the choices to be made among the many alternatives offered is becoming increasingly complex. Surely the church must give guidance here, examining with knowledgeable persons the purposes and effects and values of the options chosen, criticizing continually, and presenting constructive advice for the future. In the past the institution appeared relevant to man in a context in which he knew much less than he does now and enjoyed much less mastery over the forbidding forces of nature. Its relevance to the future must be to men who know their powers and appreciate the possibilities within their grasp. Were Galileo with us, he could state no greater challenge; he uttered it three and a half centuries ago and some listened and some did not. Conditions then made their deafness serious. Failure to hear today is unthinkable.

4

Evolution: The Ocean Says No!

Stuart E. Nevins

The subject of the age of the earth and the age of the world ocean is a matter of extreme importance. If there is evidence for an old ocean, then this could be used to support the evolutionist's supposition that life arose from primitive, inorganic marine chemicals over a billion years ago. If, however, the world ocean can be shown to be a relatively youthful feature, then the evolutionist would seem to lose his case by default.

Ocean Models

Two basic models for the world ocean can be imagined. According to evolutionary uniformitarian geologists, the earth is approximately 455 billion years old. The world ocean is supposed to have formed by outgassing of water by volcanic processes early in the earth's history. By no later than 1 billion years ago, in the popular scheme, the ocean reached its present size and chemical condition, and primitive one-celled life forms had already evolved by chance processes from lifeless chemicals. For a period of at least 1 billion years the ocean has remained at roughly constant salinity while the single-celled creatures evolved into mollusks, fish, reptiles, mammals, and finally man. During this vast period of time the continents have been eroding more or less continuously with debris being steadily deposited as sediments on the ocean floor.

An alternate to the evolutionist's view of the ocean is the creationist's view. According to the creationist, the ocean formed very recently—perhaps only 10,000 years ago. The earth in its original condition was covered with water (Gen. 1:2), but later God formed the ocean basins by gathering the waters together, allowing the dry land to appear (Gen. 1:9). The ocean again covered the earth

77

during the universal Flood in the days of Noah, and returned to their present basins following the Flood.

The purpose of this paper is to examine erosion and sedimentation rates to see who has the better model for the world ocean.

Ocean Sediments

The floor of the ocean is blanketed by a layer of poorly consolidated material called sediment. Small rock particles and precipitated chemicals derived from the continents, especially by streams, form the bulk of this sediment. Chemically precipitated calcareous ooze is the most common deep ocean sediment, while continent-derived sand and mud is most common in the shallower ocean and nearer to shore.

Deep sea drilling and seismic surveys have provided much information about the thickness of sediments in the ocean. These data were quite surprising to early oceanographers who, assuming a great age for the ocean, expected a great thickness of sediment. The average thickness of deep ocean sediments is less than 0.40 mile (2,100 feet). Greater thicknesses of sediments are encountered on the continental shelves and slopes. The best world average sediment thickness over the entire ocean (shallow and deep) would be about 0.56 mile or 2,950 feet.[1] This estimate is generous and would be accepted as approximately correct by most evolutionary-uniformitarian geologists.

We can now calculate the volume of ocean sediments simply by multiplying the average thickness (0.56 mile) by the area of the world ocean (139.4 million square miles).[2] The calculation shows that 77 million cubic miles of sediment are present on the ocean floor.

Next, we can estimate the mass of ocean sediments by multiplying the volume of sediments (77 million cubic miles) by the average sediment density (10.7 billion tons/cubic mile = 2.30 grams/cubic centimeter).[3] It will be discovered that the mass of ocean sediments is about 820 million billion tons.

The present topographic continents above sea level have a volume of about 30.4 million cubic miles and a mass of about 383 million

1. This estimate is based on the most recent data of M. Ewing, G. Carpenter, C. Windisch, and J. Ewing, "Sediment Distribution in the Oceans: The Atlantic," *Geological Society of America Bulletin* 84 (January 1973): 83. Correction was made for Pacific Ocean sediments which are not as thick on the average as Atlantic Ocean sediments.

2. John N. Holeman, "The Sediment Yield of Major Rivers of the World" *Water Resources Research* 4 (August 1968): 737.

3. The density of deep sea sediments according to several authorities averages about 2.3 grams per cubic cenimenter.

billion tons. If the present continents were eroded to sea level, about 383 million billion tons of sediment would be deposited on the ocean floor. This mass is a little less than half the mass of sediment present in today's ocean. Stated another way, it would only take the erosion of twice our present continental mass to produce today's mass of ocean sediments!

Rates of Erosion

Careful study of modern rivers on a worldwide scale shows that vast quantities of rock are being transported to the ocean. Suspended sediment, small rock particles which are carried along by river turbulence, comprise the bulk of sediment added to the ocean. The best estimate from river data suggests that 20.2 billion tons of suspended sediment enter the ocean each year.[4]

Rivers also carry dissolved chemical substances into the ocean. The chemicals are mostly bicarbonate, silica, and salts which comprise about 4.6 billion tons of sediment added to the ocean each year.[5]

Glaciers at higher latitudes are presently breaking apart and adding icebergs to the ocean. When the ice melts the entrapped sediments are deposited on the sea floor. Ice appears to be delivering about 2.2 billion tons of sediment to the ocean each year.[6]

Although little is known about the migration of fluids at great depths in the earth, water is presently being added to the oceans through the sea floor from the continents and from springs and volcanoes on the sea floor. This water also contains dissolved chemicals. A conservative estimate suggests that 0.47 billion tons of sediment are added to the ocean each year by ground waters.[7]

The seashore is constantly being worn by waves which deliver sediment to the sea. A good estimate suggests that marine erosion adds 0.28 billion tons of sediment annually.[8]

Wind-blown dust especially from desert areas and dust from volcanoes find their way to the sea. About 0.06 billion tons go into the ocean each year.[9]

Evaporation and wind remove a small amount of salts from the ocean and deposit these on the land. The amount of sediment

4. Robert M. Garrels and Fred T. Mackenzie, *Evolution of Sedimentary Rocks* (New York: W. W. Norton, 1971), pp. 104-106.

5. Ibid., pp. 102, 103.

6. Ibid., p. 110.

7. Ibid., pp. 103, 104.

8. Ibid., pp. 110, 111.

9. Ibid., p. 111.

removed in this salt spray process as aerosols is estimated at 0.29 billion tons each year.[10]

Now that we have examined the processes which deliver and remove sediment from the ocean, we are ready to calculate the total amount of sediment going into the world ocean each year. The addition of the previous erosion estimates gives a total sediment input to the ocean of 27.5 billion tons every year. This is an enormous quantity of sediment! Most evolutionary-uniformitarian geologists would admit that this total is approximately correct.

For the sake of illustration, imagine that all of this yearly sediment were loaded into railroad freight cars each having a capacity of 11 tons. We would need 2.5 billion train cars! This is a train which would extend to the moon and back 34 times! If this train were traveling past you at 60 miles per hour, it would take 32 years to pass. The sediment total shows that 80 train cars of sediment per second are being added to the ocean!

How long would it take to deliver the present continents to the ocean if the present rate of erosion continues? There are about 30.4 million cubic miles of continental crust above sea level with a mass of 383 million billion tons. To calculate the amount of time required to deliver the present continents to the ocean we need only divide the

10. Ibid., p. 108.

Table 1

SEDIMENT BUDGET OF THE WORLD OCEAN

Sediment Transportation Process	Amount of Sediment Transported (Billions of Tons per Year)
Suspended sediment in rivers	+20.2
Dissolved chemicals in rivers	+ 4.6
Ice	+ 2.2
Ground water	+ 0.47
Marine erosion	+ 0.28
Wind-blown dust	+ 0.06
Salt spray	− 0.29
TOTAL	+27.5

mass of continents above sea level by the annual rate of erosion. The calculation would be:

$$\frac{383 \text{ million billion tons}}{27.5 \text{ billion tons per year}} = 14 \text{ million years}$$

The continents are being denuded at a rate that could level them in a mere 14 million years! Yet, evolutionary-uniformitarian geologists feel certain that the continents have existed for at least 1 billion years. During this supposed interval of time the present continents could have been eroded over 70 times! Yet—miracle of miracles—the continents are still here and do not appear to have been eroded even *one* time!

Age of the Ocean

Even though the continents could be eroded and transported to the ocean in just 14 million years, assume that some mysterious uplifting process continues to raise the continents as they are eroding. How much sediment would form at present rates of erosion in one billion years? The answer is found by multiplying the annual rate of addition of sediments to the ocean (27.5 billion tons per year) by the alleged evolutionary age of the ocean (1 billion years). During 1 billion years 27.5 billion billion tons of sediment would be produced. This is enough to cover the entire ocean floor with 97,500 feet (18.5 miles) of sediment! In order to produce this colossal quantity of sediment an incredible layer of rock 200,000 feet (38 miles) thick would have to be eroded off the continents. Thus, if we assume the present rate of erosion and exposed continental volumes to have existed over the evolutionist's supposed 1-billion-year history of the world ocean, *we would expect a staggering layer of sediment almost 100,000 feet thick to cover the sea floor today!* Since such a monumental layer does not exist, it seems that evolutionists have grossly overestimated the age of the world ocean.

Another question is in order. How long would it take to deposit the present thickness of sediments on the ocean floor assuming constant rate of erosion? To obtain the answer we must divide the mass of sediment in the ocean by the yearly rate of sediment input. The calculation is:

$$\frac{820 \text{ million billion tons}}{27.5 \text{ billion tons per year}} = 30 \text{ million years}$$

In only 30 million years, *assuming constant rate of erosion,* all the ocean sediments could have accumulated. This age does not square with the over 1-billion-year age assumed by evolutionary-uniformitarian geologists.

It is important to note that according to evolutionary-uniformitarian geologists the last 30 million years were the time of considerable continental denudation. The greatly accelerated erosion rates of the late Cenozoic were climaxed by the ice age, "a time when the weather went wild."[11] Modern river floodplains show evidence that vast quantities of water once passed into the ocean, exceeding modern river discharges. Scientists who have been working in deep sea drilling of sediments were recently surprised how far back the evidences of glaciation and more humid climate go into the sedimentary record. Therefore, the assumption of constant rate of sedimentation is not valid but requires greatly increased erosion rates in the past. This increased rate of sediment input to the ocean might *decrease* the apparent age of ocean sediments calculated above by a factor of 10 to 100, making it even harder to reconcile with the evolutionary model.

While the difficulties encountered with the evolutionary model are readily apparent, the creation model is consistent with the evidence. According to the creation model, the ocean reached its present condition only after the Noachian Flood. Some of the oldest ocean sediments appear to have been deposited rapidly from debris-laden water immediately after the Flood. These sedimentary layers do not require an associated long history of continental erosion.

The most recent ocean sediments appear to have been deposited in the centuries after the Flood when the climate was quite humid and when rates of erosion were significantly greater than at present. Most of the recent ocean sediments are probably derived not from erosion of continental granite, but from sedimentary rocks. Thus, the more recent ocean sediments appear to be chiefly "recycled" and do not require a long history. It is eminently reasonable to believe in a young ocean with an age of 10,000 years or less.

The Evolutionist's Dilemma

If the world ocean is a billion years old, there should be an enormous quantity of ocean sediments. Yet, even the evolutionist is aware of the scarcity of sediments. What would be his rebuttal to the arguments presented so far?

In order to have an ocean over a billion years old yet possessing a

11. See R. W. Fairbridge's excellent discussion of late Cenozoic erosion in "Denudation," *The Encyclopedia of Geomorphology* (New York: Reinhold, 1968), pp. 261-71.

meager carpet of sediments, the evolutionist *must* have some process which constantly removes sediments from the sea floor. The first process which comes to mind is removing sediment by uplifting sea floor and returning ocean sediments to the continents. This may account for a little ocean sediment loss, but the total amount of sediments on the continents is about equal to the amount on the ocean floor. Adding all the sediments on the present continents to those in the modern ocean would still be far short of the anticipated 100,000 feet of ocean sediments which should exist if the ocean is a billion years old. This process does not solve the evolutionist's dilemma.

The second process is very ingenious. If the major quantity of sediment is not being removed from the ocean by uplifting, then the evolutionist must suppose some process which plunges deep ocean sediments into the depths of the earth! The favorite method is called "sea floor spreading," and suggests that the ocean floor is like a conveyor belt. Ocean crust is assumed to form continuously at the mid-ocean ridges, then it accumulates sediments as it slowly moves away from the ridge, and finally both crust and sediments are destroyed by remelting when dragged below ocean trenches. The best estimates by evolutionary-uniformitarian geologists suggest that about 2.75 billion tons of sediment per year are being destroyed by the sea floor spreading.[12] This rate is only one tenth the modern rate of addition of sediments to the ocean. Stated another way, ocean sediments are forming today at a rate ten times faster than they are being destroyed by sea floor spreading! Thus, sea floor spreading is not able to destroy sediments fast enough.

After careful analysis of the erosion of continents and associated sedimentation in the world ocean, we must ask two urgent questions. Where is all the sediment if, as the evolutionist assumes, the ocean is over one billion years old? Who has the better model for the ocean—the evolutionist or the creationist? We feel confident that the true answers concerning the origin of the ocean are presented in Scripture. "The sea is his, and he made it" (Ps. 95:5).

12. Y. Li, "Geochemical Mass Balance Among Lithosphere, Hydrosphere, and Atmosphere," *American Journal of Science* 272 (February 1972): 133.

5

Tracing the Past:
Is Uniformity Meaningful?

Loren C. Steinhauer

Each of us is accustomed to making certain extrapolations; this is a practical necessity in many spheres of daily life. For example a businessman extrapolates on the basis of current trends and then decides when to spend money and when to save it, using safety factors and varying degrees of discretion, depending on his nature. Occasionally people make extrapolations that are of questionable value—or safety. Ideally the motorist driving through a heavy rainstorm drives at a speed allowing him to stop safely within the distance of reduced visibility. But drivers in a hurry often discard the rule; they assume that if the roadway within their visibility has no obstacles, then neither will that beyond it. This is true most of the time, but the exceptions make it an unwarranted and hazardous extrapolation.

Extrapolations are made in many areas of life, and science is one of them. In truth, science is based on the fundamental extrapolation that natural laws have operated for some time in the past and will for some time in the future. This assumption of "uniformity" is at the very foundation of science; without it science would be chaotic, and hopeless. The crank and the dreamer could claim the same authority as the serious scientist for their explanations of erratic natural phenomena. Without the assurance of some sort of uniformity, science could not exist as it does now.

Nevertheless it is possible for the assumption of uniformity to be overextended and overextrapolated, leading to a simplistic or even grossly inaccurate view of the universe. This is indeed the case when scientists propose that those process rates and conditions presently observable have always operated in the same way or with the same intensity. The same may be said for rigorously insisting that the very natural laws themselves have always been in force. These extrapolations are known collectively as uniformitarianism, which grew out of the philosophy of naturalism. Uniformitarianism has been the popular approach to understanding Earth history[1] for at least 150 years. It embodies the extrapolation of presently observed processes and laws into the indefinite past (and future).

I propose that the uniformitarian assumptions are overextrapolations which have led to many erroneous conclusions. This suggestion is portrayed symbolically in figure 1. A scientist peers into the mists and concludes by extrapolation that the tail is that of an innocuous garden snake, while in fact it belongs to a ferocious dragon. If we reject the scientist's system of extrapolation, then we must be prepared to give him a better one with which to discover what kind of animal the tail actually belongs to. Likewise if the presuppositions of uniformitarianism are to be discarded, they must

1. *Earth history* is the history of all physical events of planet Earth since its origin. It is to be distinguished from human history except where man affects Earth history or records it.

Fig. 1. The overextrapolations of uniformitarian scientists

be replaced by a superior set, one which is consistent with both the real world and scriptural principles.

The Popular Approach to Earth History

Scientific hypothesis: appearing before the court. The function of science is to assemble facts, build hypotheses, and experimentally test these hypotheses. The importance of the check system—testing —cannot be minimized. Any theory must be subjected to rigorous testing; it must meet the criterion of "reproducibility of observation." Science must never be cut loose from the restraint of the test because the inevitable result would be the appearance of a multitude of speculative theories, limited by little more than the imaginations of their creators. Without a system of testing, no one can say objectively that a theory is valid or invalid. This was the error of Descartes and Leibnitz, who generated seemingly endless speculations on the nature of the world system.[2] For example, Descartes (a brilliant French mathematician of the seventeenth century) produced an exotic theory of planetary motions, but he simply refused to test it with the detailed and readily available observations of Kepler. A. d'Abro has remarked: "What condemns Descartes is his utter disregard for facts."[3] Indeed if a hypothesis is valid, it should survive repeated testing. If it does not, it should be molded, bent, or discarded to accommodate the facts. As someone has quipped, the history of science is full of stubborn, ugly little facts that destroy beautiful theories.

Science and history: an unhappy marriage? We have seen that science necessarily involves extrapolation: laws demonstrable in the present have been in effect for some time in the past and will persist for some time in the future. However, when science moves into the realm of history, this basic assumption becomes inadequate; there is an enormous difference between trying to discover *laws* in effect in the past and attempting to trace *events* that actually took place. It has been charged that the study of Earth history is not strictly a science, since it lies outside the scope of the scientific method.[4] The argument is that a particular event in Earth history is absolutely non-repeatable; it is once and for all; no theory about that event can meet the criterion of "reproducibility of observation."

It is not fair to make the blanket accusation that Earth-history

---

2. A. d'Abro, *The Rise of the New Physics*, 2nd ed., 2 vols. (New York: Dover, 1951), 1:11, 12.

3. Ibid., p. 1.

4. Henry M. Morris, "Science Versus Scientism in Historical Geology," in *A Symposium on Creation* (Grand Rapids: Baker, 1968), p. 12.

scientists have forgotten about testing; the fact is that testing in the familiar sense is simply impossible. Actually, credit must be given for the increasing effort devoted to "model testing" in recent years. Model testing is the construction of a small scale model which is put through a test to simulate this or that process or event. Yet even this approach is only testing by proxy. The results are conclusive only in that they judge the physical possibility of a theorized process, and not whether it actually did occur at some point in history. I intend not to minimize the importance of model testing but only to point out its limitations.

Thus the student of Earth history is severely limited. Lacking the mythical "time machine," he cannot observe again, repeatedly, an event that has already happened.[5] If he is to learn anything, he must assume some degree of continuity with the past and thus provide an organized system for testing theories of historical events. This assumption amounts to an extrapolation from the present backward in time. The study of Earth history, then, involves two basic extrapolative assumptions: present mathematical and physical principles were valid in the past; and there is sufficient continuity between present and past events to allow for testing.

Two such assumptions form the basis of the famous principle of uniformity, popularized by Charles Lyell 150 years ago. Ruth Moore described Lyell's position: "The present is the key to the past. . . . No causes whatever have from the earliest time . . . to the present, ever acted, but those now acting: and they have never acted with different degrees of energy from that which they now exert."[6]

Geologist Stephen J. Gould recently elucidated the principle of uniformity and clearly distinguished between its two parts. The former he labeled *methodological uniformitarianism,* "a procedural principle asserting spatial and temporal invariance of natural laws" (essentially a corollary of naturalism), and the latter, *substantive uniformitarianism,* "a testable theory of geological change postulating uniformity of rates or material conditions."[7]

We have seen that Earth history deals with historic events which cannot be directly tested in the present. This limitation necessitates assumptions which will allow for an alternate mode of testing. One such assumption is provided by the principle of uniformity which extrapolates both present natural laws and present process rates into

5. Model testing does not amount to an exact reproduction of the event because every such test involves several unprovable assumptions about the original event.

6. *The Earth We Live On* (New York: Knopf, 1911), pp. 145, 146. It should be noted that the principle of uniformity will admit local deviations in the rate of a process, and even local catastrophes, but it will allow no such disturbances on a global scale.

7. "Is Uniformitarianism Necessary?" *American Journal of Science* 263 (1965): 223.

the indefinite past. In this scheme a theory is tested by examining in the present the experimental results and the physical evidences in the universe, and linking them to the past using current process rates. This is the significance of the statement: "The present is the key to the past."

The question naturally arises: Are the presuppositions of uniformitarianism acceptable? More fundamentally: What *is* the criterion for an acceptable set of presuppositions? The only reasonable answer seems to be that given by theologian Francis Schaeffer: ". . . presuppositions are selected on the basis of which presuppositions fit what is; that is, what presuppositions give solid answers concerning what is. . . . in regard to the universe and in regard to man."[8] The assumptions of uniformitarianism will be examined for their consistency with the universe as it is, and with man as he is.

The credo of the uniformitarian: a great leap. A definitive position in any sphere of life must ultimately be based on a fundamental set of axioms or presuppositions. Moreover, a given position can be no stronger than the presuppositions upon which it is based. In the following discussion the two presuppositions of uniformitarianism are examined: one is at variance with observation; the other, though correlating with many observations, leads to logical and philosophical contradictions.

Consider the assumption of substantive uniformitarianism that *process rates* and *material conditions* are uniform and invariant when viewed on a global scale. First of all it must be recognized that process rates do indeed depend on material conditions: as the latter vary, so do the former. Geologist Stuart E. Nevins has observed: "Actually, the assumption that process rates must be uniform is without scientific backing. There is no scientific law which requires a natural event always to proceed at a constant rate. A scientific law only describes an event under a fixed set of conditions and as conditions vary, so does the rate. Conditions, not scientific law, determine the rate of a process."[9] One example is human population growth. Under a fixed set of conditions—sociological attitudes toward childbirth, family size, and the value of human life; the state of medical knowledge; economic wealth or famine; war or peace; epidemics; natural disasters and so on—the net growth rate will be

8. *The Church at the End of the 20th Century* (Downers Grove, Ill.: Inter-Varsity, 1970), pp. 23, 24.

9. "A Scriptural Groundwork for Historical Geology," in *Symposium on Creation II*, ed. Donald W. Patten (Grand Rapids: Baker, 1970), p. 88.

constant. But a change in even one of these "conditions" may cause a major alteration of the net growth rate.[10]

The question, then, is whether material conditions have been invariant on a global scale. Again pursuing the example of human population growth, we observe that during history there *have* been significant changes in the growth rate, resulting from changes in material conditions. Furthermore, these changes have occurred on a global level. There is also evidence of major changes in the physical condition of earth, rapid—even abrupt—changes, disturbances, and great discontinuities. These discontinuities involve changes which cannot possibly fit into the framework of current process rates.

In addition to changes in material conditions, there is the ever-present possibility (usually probability) of unknown factors. Nevins continues: "Factors may exist which scientists have not yet discovered. To insist that present rates or material conditions are average for all geological time rests entirely upon uniformitarian assumption."[11] This makes the candid uniformitarian very uneasy. William M. Davis, for example, commented forcefully: "The very foundation of our science is only an inference: for the whole of it rests on the unprovable assumption that all through the inferred lapse of time which the inferred performance of inferred geological processes involves, they have been going on in a manner consistent with the laws of nature as we know them now." Davis concludes: "We seldom realize the magnitude of that assumption."[12] Indeed it is a titanic extrapolation, a blind leap of faith that contradicts what is observable in the universe. A few scientists have recently become aware of this leap and abandoned it.

Despite the departure of many from substantive uniformitarianism, most scientists continue to cling to methodological uniformitarianism, the concept of invariant natural laws with no divine intervention. This seems consistent with nature, which is law abiding and exhibits marvelous orderliness. Indeed, were it not for some sort of uniformity of natural law, science in the modern sense

10. The spontaneous decay of radioactive isotopes appears to be an exception, for it seems to proceed quite independently of physical conditions. The decay rates may indeed be constant. Yet the conditions under which they are known to be constant may not be all the conditions experienced by the isotope during its life. For example, can we be certain that the decay has always been spontaneous, or has there been at some point stimulated decay? Robert V. Gentry has suggested that radioactive decay rates may have changed greatly during geologic time. He is quoted in Donald E. Chittick, "Dating the Earth and Fossils," in *Symposium on Creation II*, pp. 68, 69.

11. "A Scriptural Groundwork for Historical Geology," p.88.

12. "The Value of Outrageous Geological Hypothesis," *Science* 63 (May 7, 1926): 465, 466.

could never have been born. Yet, methodological uniformitarianism can lead to great contradictions. The first instance involves the whole question of origins. Two star witnesses have often been called forth to testify against the strict invariance of natural law: the first and second laws of thermodynamics. The *first* law (conservation of mass-energy) is clearly violated if one suggests that our universe had a beginning. Original creation is a nonconservative process with something being made out of nothing. Furthermore, if one chooses to deny an origin (by supposing the universe has always existed) the *second* law is violated. An infinitely old universe would long ago have suffered what has been called "heat death," in which all ordered structures are reduced to the ultimate depth of randomness and disorder. This is clearly not the state of the universe today.[13]

The whole question of origins and the related question of miracles are classic in science. Concerned scientists have grappled with them for centuries. A truce is often reached by concluding that miracles and origins lie *outside* the realm of science, hence are not of vital concern to the scientist since he does not face these in his daily work. This position is only begging the question and does *not* free one to hold presuppositions which forbid origins or miracles. Simply calling something "nonscience" does not make it nonsense or unimportant.

The second instance in which methodological uniformitarianism leads to a contradiction is the nature of man. Assuming invariant natural laws without divine intervention turns the whole of nature into a large, complex machine. Moreover, the logical conclusion of this position is that nature holds not merely physics in its sway, but everything, including the very souls of men (supposing man can have a soul in such a context). Man is caught in the gears of a huge deterministic machine which turns him according to its own unbending rule. Schaeffer has drawn the logical conclusion with regard to human significance: "Everything is in the machine. No longer physics only; now psychology and social science are also in the machine. Freedom does not exist. In fact love no longer exists; significance, in the old sense of man longing for significance, no longer exists."[14]

This is a dismal conclusion that few uniformitarian scientists have dared to face directly, even though it is the logical result of their assumptions. And so they hang suspended between the presuppositions which they refuse to give up and the logical conclusions

13. Some have sought to make an "end run" around the second law of thermodynamics by calling for an indefinite series of cycles in the universe in which all order is not lost. Yet this requires periods in which order is being regained, hence violating the second law.

14. *Escape from Reason* (Downers Grove, Ill.: Inter-Varsity, 1968), p. 37.

which they refuse to face. Herein lies the philosophical contradiction of methodological uniformitarianism. The one who embraces this axiom sooner or later finds that he cannot live in a manner consistent with his presupposition. Schaeffer cited the noted existentialist philosopher, Jean Paul Sartre, as an example. Sartre has logically concluded from his presuppositions that there is no ultimate meaning; hence nothing can be right or wrong. And yet when laying down his pen, he moves out into the world where he really lives and violates his own philosophy. For example he has condemned the United States for immoral and criminal actions in Vietnam. Sartre is holding a philosophy which he cannot live and his dilemma is very clear.[15]

The philosophical despair that arises out of uniformitarian axioms is unnecessary; there need not be a tension between one's philosophy and one's way of life, or between one's philosophy and the universe as it is. But one must discard the false presuppositions in favor of others that "are selected on the basis of which presupposition fits what is; that is, what presuppositions give solid answers concerning what is. It is only the Christian presuppositions which explain what is—in regard to the universe and in regard to man."[16]

An Anchor Point in Scripture

One might think that discarding the popular principle of uniformity casts the whole of Earth-history science on the rocks, robbing the past of any sort of continuity with the present. One might think that without uniformity we can never be certain what did happen in the past, thus threatening the very basis of Earth history. Yet it *is* possible to learn much about past events. The basis for our knowledge is the principle of uniformity found in Scripture.

The scriptural theme: a law-abiding universe. Before we can begin to examine nature, we must be assured that some definable sort of uniformity is operating in the universe. Indeed an order and regularity are obvious to any observer. The naturalist sees it and concludes, "The same causes generate the same effects," which is indeed true. But the naturalist errs when he adds: "The same causes generate the same effects in the closed system of material universe."

Scripture teaches the uniformity of natural causes but not the closed system of the material universe. Consider figure 2. Below the heavy line is the material universe, divided into two parts: the governing natural laws, and the actual space-time course of events in the material substance. The naturalist acknowledges only what is

15. *The God Who is There* (Downers Grove, Ill.: Inter-Varsity, 1968), pp. 56, 123, 124.
16. *The Church at the End of the 20th Century,* pp. 23, 24.

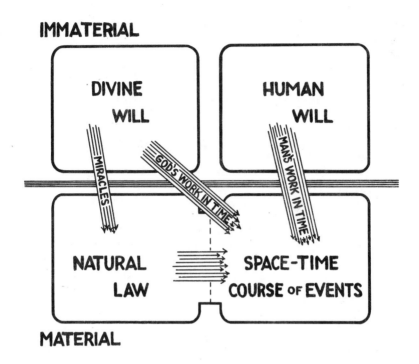

Fig. 2. Uniformity of natural causes, but not a closed system

below the heavy line and places human will in the box with space-time events. Thus he admits only those causes represented by the arrows from the natural law to the events. But Scripture teaches that there are causes from nonmaterial sources, including God and created intelligences (human and angelic). Now we see more causal arrows: the divine will interrupts natural laws (miracles) and also causes events in space-time history. Likewise, human will causes events in history. In an age when determinism is popular, it is indeed comforting to realize that human will can actually affect history.

Now we are prepared to formulate the first presupposition, scriptural uniformity: *There is a uniformity of natural causes in the universe and the causes fall into four categories: operation of natural law (which is upheld by God),*[17] *operation of divine will to suspend natural law, operation of divine will to alter the course of history, and operation of human (and angelic) will to alter the course of history.* A corollary is that God sus-

17. ". . . by him [the Son of God] all things consist" (Col. 1:17); the Son of God is "upholding all things by the word of his power" (Heb. 1:3).

pends natural law only very rarely and for specific purposes.[18] The regularity of natural law testifies to the faithfulness and immutability of God.[19] But the fact of occasional miracles testifies to God's power over natural law. God is constantly at work in history but only rarely resorts to suspending natural law.[20] This corollary, then, should read: *Biblical events should be regarded as consistent with natural laws unless the Bible itself says otherwise; extrabiblical events which, according to available information, violate natural law, should be regarded as "candidates" for the status of miracle, to be continually reviewed in the light of new information.*

A note of caution must be sounded in regard to labeling a given event a miracle. Christians have been prone to identify "unexplainable" events as miracles, events which violated natural laws. This has often led to embarrassment when newly discovered natural laws readily explain what was previously beyond explanation. Thus the above corollary cautiously refers to apparent miracles as candidates. One should first search diligently for an explanation in the sphere of natural law. This is the usual approach of an experimentalist confronted by an errant data point; he does not immediately cry out "Miracle!" but rather searches for the cause in some irregular factor.

Observing the past: untapped storehouse. Having adopted the scriptural principle of uniformity, we are prepared to attack the problem of how to learn about actual events of the past. To understand a historical event in a scientific sense one must establish a continuity between past and present. This continuity must also form the basis for testing theories of historical events. The presupposition of substantive uniformitarianism, because it is based on a faulty extrapolation, must be discarded, but what is to replace it? The answer lies in a perspective given by the scriptural principle of uniformity: the interplay between human and divine wills can have many profound

18. Angelic beings can also interfere with the laws of nature, although only on a limited scale (II Thess. 2:9; Rev. 13:4, 12, 13). God chose to severely restrict angelic interference in order to maintain regularity in the universe and thus to display His faithfulness.

19. The Old Testament refers many times to regularity in nature and clearly links this to the faithfulness of God (Job 38:33, Ps. 89:2, 5, 37; 119:89-91; 148:6; Jer. 31:35, 36; 33:25). The biblical concept of the regularity of nature is discussed in Bernard Ramm, *The Christian View of Science and Scripture* (Grand Rapids: Eerdmans, 1966), pp. 85, 88. Ramm summarizes the more extensive work, E. C. Rust, *Nature and Man in Biblical Thought* (London: Lutterworth, 1953).

20. Jesus Christ illustrated this during His earthly ministry. He worked many miracles, but He used great discretion. He often declined to perform a miracle when he could accomplish His purpose by natural means. He was capable of walking on water, but Scripture reports only one instance of it; the rest of the time He rode in boats, taking advantage of the law of bouyancy.

effects on the course of Earth history. Thus the student of Earth history must search out much more than mere marks on the Earth of past events, he must also look into the recorded history of God and man to discover where they have affected and been affected by natural events on Earth. This suggests three basic sources of information: divine revelation in the Scripture, human records, and physical evidences in the universe. These three records form the raw data from which one can both learn of historic events and test one's theories about them.

The second basic presupposition then links past to present and might be called the "continuity of knowledge." It may be stated as follows: *One can observe* in the present *records which were made* in the past *to derive systematically a true and meaningful interpretation. The interpretation forms the basis for subsequent theory building and testing.* Note the fundamental difference between this assumption and that of ordinary scientific observation, in which one assumes he can observe (in the present) events taking place in the present and derive a true interpretation. Note also that the statement only asserts a general principle and of course does not specify the rules for finding a true and meaningful interpretation. The large issue of hermeneutics (for each of the three categories of records) is beyond the scope of this article, but a passing comment is in order. Hermeneutics of divine and human records must be largely divorced from the natural sciences, because interpretations of records should not be forced to conform to a contemporary and possibly erroneous understanding of the universe.

Sadly enough, scientific investigation of Earth history (at least for 150 years) has largely ignored two of the three sources. This "oversight" is due partly to the fact that human records and the divine record contain numerous references to events (catastrophes, miracles) which do not fit uniformitarian presuppositions, and which uniformitarians consequently have discarded as erroneous. But what an error to discard two-thirds of the available evidence. Indeed, the courageous scientist should not merely observe the tail (fig. 1) and compute great extrapolations, but should also make the record speak to him by giving the tail a pull—and then be prepared to face the consequences. This is science as it should be: giving consideration to all sources of information even though they may threaten vested interests: one's own theories.

The preferred hypothesis. Part of the application of "continuity of knowledge" involves testing a theory. Testing was shown to be an indispensable part of science, without which theories "run free" and wild, divergent speculation ensues. The basic substance for the test is furnished by data in the three types of records. The test itself must consist of simple criteria or ground rules.

There are perhaps many ways in which one may arrange the ground rules for judging a hypothesis, but the following concise system of four is particularly lucid. (1) *Accountability*. The preferred hypothesis must best account for the interpretation drawn from the available records. (2) *Coordination*. The preferred hypothesis must best coordinate and connect diverse elements in the records. For example, it should explain apparent chance coincidences linking seemingly unrelated elements in the records. (3) *Predictability*. The preferred hypothesis must agree with subsequent discoveries of new records. It should also direct research in such a way as to lead to new discoveries, in the areas of both theory and records. (4) *Simplicity*. "When a natural event can be described in several different ways, the principle of simplicity merely states that the scientist should first consider the simplest description which agrees with the available evidence."[21]

Certainty and doubt in science: judicious flexibility. There is a curious verse in the Bible on knowledge: "If anyone supposes that he knows anything, he has not yet known as he ought to know" (I Cor. 8:2, *New American Standard*). The man who supposes he has definite knowledge on a given subject must realize that his understanding, though it seems to him complete and "airtight," may yet be vastly incomplete, emphasizing the wrong thing or being just plain wrong. There will always be a certain amount of doubt about any scientific theory. Who is certain that an experiment performed 100 times with consistent results will yield the same on the 101st try? D'Abro stated the proper response of the scientist: "If we are ultra cautious and refuse to generalize, experiment becomes useless since it cannot be used as a source of more general knowledge. Faced with the alternative of choosing safety with sterility or doubt with possible progress, the physicist adopts the same course as does the layman in his daily activities; he relinquishes safety and he generalizes."[22] This generalization (scientific induction) is sufficient in the sphere of natural law but not in the sphere of historical events, where another fundamental assumption (continuity of knowledge) must be included. Another assumption introduces more doubts. Thus, theories of historical events must be developed with great care, and one must be prepared to abandon them in part or altogether if subsequent information so requires. This is frequently not done, according to the astronomer Guy de Vaucouleurs: "I am concerned

21. "A Scriptural Groundwork for Historical Geology," p. 98.

22. *The Rise of the New Physics*, p. 16.

by an apparent loss of contact with empirical evidence and observational facts, and worse, by a deliberate refusal on the part of some theorists to accept such results when they appear in conflict with some of the present oversimplified and therefore intellectually appealing theories of the universe."[23]

Thus we must maintain the position that there will always be a degree of doubt about any hypothesis; the hypothesis may in the end prove to be false, or only a rough approximation of the actual event. Bernard Ramm summarized the issue: "Among scientists 'true science' means 'the best we have to date as developed by our best scientists.' In this sense 'true science' is not infallible."[24]

Form and freedom in science: a plea for liberty. It is fitting to close this discussion with a few remarks on the latitude permitted the scientist in pursuit of discovery. Earlier, the necessity of scientific testing was shown. Testing is simply a *form*, a restraint upon scientific theory; the removal of this form leads to the excesses previously mentioned. There is also another form, a moral one, and freedom from this moral form also leads to excesses. We are witnessing today the excesses of science, wed to technology, cut loose and running free. It is ruining our environment. Science, then, must operate within both forms.

But there is also freedom within these forms. This is the freedom to probe freely—even recklessly—the unknown. It is freedom in that the unknown may be explored by imaginative departures from the old classical routines. There is a pitfall, to be sure: Descartes perverted his liberty by refusing to be subject to the restraints of the test. But there is the equally great danger of being overrestrictive and stifling progress. Charles Sanders Pierce has said, and history concurs: "Every plank of advance is first laid . . . by the spontaneous conjectures of instinctive reason."

Such imaginative conjecture can lead to momentous discoveries in Earth-history science as it has in other sciences. We dare not shy away from the novel and innovative simply because they threaten popular ideas. This is science in the best sense: reaching down and pulling the tail of the dragon even though the consequences are uncertain.

23. "The Case for a Hierarchical Cosmology," *Science* 167 (February 27, 1970): 1203.
24. *The Christian View of Science and Scripture*, p. 42.

6

The Case for Global Catastrophism

Loren C. Steinhauer

Few experiences are more gripping than that of the courtroom. The pomp, the flowing robes of the judge, the pounding gavel, the booming voice of the bailiff, the buzz of the audience—all create an aura of pageantry. Simultaneously, the nervous defendant, the flash and oratory of the prosecuting attorney, the compassion of his opponent—build an air of intrigue and suspense. Even the very words spoken contribute to the scene: wit and sarcasm; heated diatribe and cool rejoinder; the indignation; the railing; pathos and bathos. And yet none of these is the real substance of a trial; the real substance is the witnesses themselves and their testimony. Strip away all the pomp and routine and you still have a trial. Strip away the witnesses and nothing is left.

Many witnesses may be called during the course of a trial: eye-witnesses who have actually observed this or that; written witnesses such as letters and contracts; and objects, physical evidence such as the supposed "murder weapon." Indeed, all available witnesses are called in order to build the most convincing case. The composite testimony will contain at least seeming contradictions: some arise simply from variant vantage points, others from false testimony. Each witness is examined and cross-examined to determine the validity of his account.

The courtroom ordeal is not limited to the legal profession; it enters into other endeavors, and science is one of them. In particular, the study of Earth history[1] involves a courtroom-like drama to uncover the truth about supposed historical events. Here the ter-

1. *Earth history* is the history of all physical events of planet Earth since its origin. It is to be distinguished from human history except where man affects Earth history or records it.

minology is different—a theory is being built and tested—but the process is essentially the same: witnesses must be examined to build the case, and then they must be cross-examined to test it. A case is built upon the testimony of several witnesses to describe the overall character of Earth history.

The thesis of global catastrophism is this: the last 2600 years of Earth history have been peaceful, the only physical catastrophes (flooding rivers, violent storms, volcanic eruptions, and so forth) having been strictly local in scale and not worldwide in any real sense; in contrast, the period from the creation of Earth to about 700 B.C. was marked by several violent catastrophes of worldwide impact wrought largely by extraterrestrial causes. These great convulsions were generally expressions of divine wrath upon human wickedness. The following discussion will draw on available "witnesses" to support this hypothesis.

If global catastrophism is on trial, so is uniformitarianism, and in particular substantive uniformitarianism, which presupposes that Earth has had a peaceful history devoid of any global catastrophe. In "Tracing the Past: Is Uniformity Meaningful," I showed the inability of uniformitarian presuppositions to account for many things. This article builds the case for a theory which is in total contradiction with uniformitarianism. Hence, if global catastrophism is established (and strong evidence supports it), it demonstrates the pitiful inadequacy of uniformitarianism to give a true picture of Earth history.

Examining the Witnesses

The case for global catastrophism is built upon the testimony of several witnesses: the divine record (Scripture), human records, and physical evidences in the universe. Before calling for the testimony, we must establish the general qualifications of the witnesses and the proper way to interpret their testimony.

The first source of information is Scripture, which provides two different categories of facts. Scripture gives unique information on the operation of divine will in the universe, the purposes and objectives of the Creator in space-time events. The Bible does not indicate the mechanics by which God brought about an event, but it usually reveals His purpose. The Bible is also a source of historical data. A comment on the qualifications of human writers of Scripture is necessary. Some immediately dismiss the value of the biblical record as a source of data because of the "nonscientific background" of the human writers. It may rather be argued that the "nonscientific" writer of Scripture recorded exactly what he saw (the eyeball approach) in contrast to a modern scientist who may discard some bit of information if it does not fit into his scheme. The objectivity of Bible history is demonstrated by the many embarrassing events which the human author included, even when it might have been in his own interest to delete it.

The Bible, like any record, requires proper interpretation. The interpretation of Scripture has been a subject of great controversy, but it seems that the only reasonable method is the literal, or grammatical-historical method defined by Bernard Ramm: "The literal method of interpretation is that method that gives to each word the same basic meaning it would have in normal, ordinary, customary usage, whether employed in writing, speaking or thinking."[2] In another work Ramm discusses the language of the Bible with reference to natural things.[3]

The second source of information is human records, including all written history except the Bible, recorded mythologies, and archaeological artifacts. Ancient writers, like the biblical writers, used the eyeball approach, writing down what they saw. Thus it is reasonable to use something akin to the grammatical-historical method of interpretation. Regarding the qualifications of the ancient observers, it must be noted that there are many known instances in which they recorded events with great accuracy. Indeed, the Chaldean and Egyptian astronomers made very accurate observations, and Hipparchus, a Greek, actually discovered the minute precision of the equinoxes in the second century B.C. Recognizing the accuracy of the ancients over against the massive extrapolation in modern science, Rene Gallant asked: "One of the two must be wrong! Which? The ancient people who described what they saw, or the astronomers whose calculations were made 4,500 years later? The testimony of eye-witnesses in Antiquity may not be so lightly disregarded!"[4]

Human literature does not, however, possess the same authority as divine revelation; the latter is inerrant as given by God, while the former is subject to error. Therefore even greater care must be exercised in interpreting human records, especially the myths which may contain only a grain of truth in the midst of a volume of untrue trappings. Myths are the victims of substantial transmission errors, the transmitters throwing in interpretations or even embellishments. Frequently, particularly in myths, false ideas about the *cause* of an event have crept in. Therefore, to interpret a myth one must carefully distinguish actual observation from suggested cause. A good check system on mythologies is that of correlation: if myths from several distant cultures describe the same event, without unreasonable variations, then one may conclude that the event is indeed historical.

2. *Protestant Biblical Interpretation* (Boston: W. A. Wilde, 1950), p. 53.

3. *The Christian View of Science and Scripture* (Grand Rapids: Eerdmans, 1966), pp. 65-80.

4. *Bombarded Earth* (London: John Baker, 1964), p. 148.

The third source of information is physical evidence in the universe. This is an important source but is in many ways the weakest; it only gives the present remains of past events. The physical evidence at a point on the Earth at the present instant is the sum total of all the events that have happened down through history at that local point, and summations tend to sweep many details into oblivion. Nevertheless, physical evidence may often be the only record available, and even when eyewitness accounts are known, physical evidences become invaluable as correlations for testing one's theory of a historical event.

Testimony of the Witnesses

The Scripture: divine wrath amid divine faithfulness. God has a stake in the regularity of natural law and the orderly function of nature; these things stand as ever present testimonies of His faithfulness. But God has also demonstrated His ability to suspend the general course of nature. His interjections usually took place entirely in the sphere of natural law; a miracle is not necessary to perpetrate a catastrophe, even a global one. This is particularly clear when extraterrestrial materials are involved. One must not think, though, that God has never resorted to miracles—suspensions of natural law. Numerous examples are recorded in Scripture, particularly in the early ministry of Jesus Christ. These interruptions were not the random, pointless play of a fickle deity but the intentional expression of God's righteous wrath upon wickedness: "Fire goes before Him, and burns up His adversaries round about. His lightnings lit up the world; the earth saw and trembled. The mountains melted like wax at the presence of the LORD. At the presence of the LORD of the whole earth. The heavens declare His righteousness, and all the peoples have seen His glory" (Ps. 97:3-6).[5] The same theme is sung in Job 9:6, Psalm 18:7, and Jeremiah 10:10.

Consider some of the catastrophes recorded in Scripture:

1. The Flood (Gen. 6-8) was the expression of God's judgment on the wickedness of man in Noah's day (II Peter 2:5; Gen. 6:5-7). The Genesis account suggests the Flood was global in scope: ". . . all the high mountains were covered . . . and all flesh perished . . . and all mankind." (Gen. 7:19-21)

2. Sodom and Gomorrah (Gen. 18, 19) were two ancient cities destroyed by a judgment from God (Gen. 18:20; II Peter 2:6; Jude 7). Their demise was awesome: "The LORD rained on Sodom and Gomorrah brimstone and fire from the LORD out of heaven . . . the smoke of the land ascended like the smoke of a furnace" (Gen.

5. Scripture quotations throughout this article are from the *New American Standard Bible*.

19:24, 28). "He condemned the cities of Sodom and Gomorrah to destruction by reducing them to ashes" (II Peter 2:6). Their destruction was from space, involving falling fiery stones.

3. The exodus (Exod. 8-19) of Israel from Egypt was accompanied by numerous great catastrophes, including the plagues (judgment on the Egyptians), the parting of the Red Sea and its return (also judgment), and the upheaval at Sinai (revelation). Some of the disturbances were from space: " . . . thunder, hail, and fire . . . rained on the land of Egypt" (Exod. 9:23). As for Sinai, it was but a visible revelation of the awesome power of God, "being all in smoke because the LORD descended upon it in fire and its smoke ascended like the smoke of a furnace, and the whole mountain quaked violently" (Exod. 19:18).

4. The fall of Jericho (Josh. 6) was a divine judgment on disobedience (Heb. 11:31), perpetrated as "the walls fell down flat" (Josh. 6:20).

5. Joshua's long day (Josh. 10) saw the execution of divine judgment on the armies of Canaan, through the armies of Israel and meteoritic materials. In the process God disturbed the motion or apparent motion of the sun so that the battle could be carried to a decisive conclusion. The altering of the sun's motion suggests an extraterrestrial cause, as do the associated phenomena: ". . .the LORD threw large stones from heaven on them . . . there were more who died from the hailstones than those whom the sons of Israel killed with the sword" (Josh. 10:11).

6. The dial of Ahaz incident (Isa. 38; II Kings 20) also involved the disturbance of the sun's apparent motion (and perhaps the Earth's spin axis). It was a deliverance, not a judgment, and an indication that God had heard the prayer of Hezekiah for an extended life. Again an extraterrestrial source for the disturbance seems to be the simplest explanation.[6]

7. Numerous catastrophes are referred to in Scripture, among them: the Earth shaking (Ps. 18:7; 60:2; 97:4; 104:32; 114:7; Heb. 12:26), the last reference clearly saying that the whole Earth shook; mountains shaking and moving (Job 9:5; Ps. 18:7; 114:4); mountains melting or extruding lava (Ps. 97:5); the heavens moving (II Sam. 22:8; Job 26:11), suggesting a disturbance in or from space; the Earth moving out of place (Ps. 82:5), indicating a global disturbance from space; the times and seasons changing (Dan. 2:21, 22), also indicating a global disturbance from space. Thus we may conclude that Scripture clearly testifies of several catastrophes in his-

6. The problem of whether Joshua's long day and Ahaz's dial were interruptions (or precessions) of the Earth's spinning motion has stirred much controversy. The problem is resolved in: Donald W. Patten, Ronald R. Hatch, and Loren C. Steinhauer, *The Long Day of Joshua* (Seattle: Pacific Meridian, 1973).

tory, some of which are global in scope and extraterrestrial in cause. Scripture also teaches that behind the catastrophes was the purposeful expression of divine judgment on wickedness, or in at least one case, the revelation of God's awesome power to His people Israel.

It should also be noted that many prophetic passages foresaw global upheavals involving extraterrestrial phenomena, which are the judgments of God. Since this work deals with historical events, these passages will not be listed, save one of particular significance. The apostle Peter warns against mocking future, catastrophic, divine judgments: "Know this first of all, that in the last days mockers will come with their mocking . . . and saying, 'Where is the promise of His coming? For ever since the fathers fell asleep, all continues just as it was from the beginning of creation.' For when they maintain this, it escapes their notice that by the word of God the heavens existed long ago and the earth was formed out of water and by water, through which the world at that time was destroyed, being flooded with water" (II Peter 3:3-6).

Human records: danger in the skies. Human records describing the era since about 700 B.C. picture a rather peaceful environment for man, but those describing more ancient times offer ample testimony to several great cataclysms of global scope, extraterrestrial origin, and severe intensity. These ancient records have been the object of much modern research, and what follows is only a summary of the data that has been accumulated.

1. Traditions of periodic catastrophes were common among the ancients. Most of the ancient philosophers believed that Earth experienced periodic worldwide disasters which dramatically altered its face, nearly annihilating life. Immanuel Velikovsky listed several ancient philosophers and philosophies that "believed in periodic conflagrations by which the world was consumed and shaped anew."[7] He also listed ancient cultures from every corner of the globe who believed in "world ages" separated by catastrophes. Most if not all of these traditions are classified as mythology. But while they contain a lot of imaginative appendages, they also contain much truth which must be drawn out. This becomes apparent when one hears the chorus of voices from widely separated and seemingly unrelated civilizations calling together for peaceful world ages punctuated by worldwide destruction. The voices of mythologies

7. *Worlds in Collision* (New York: Doubleday, 1950), pp. 29-35. A comment is in order concerning Velikovsky. He is controversial partly because he is a catastrophist instead of a uniformitarian and partly because his theories seem fanciful, incapable of reasonable physical explanation. But his inability to construct meaningful physical theories should not reflect upon his ability to assemble great masses of ancient records that point toward catastrophes.

are supported by another branch of human records, archaeological stratigraphy, which according to C. F. A. Schaeffer points conclusively toward a series of contemporaneous downfalls of civilizations throughout Eurasia. Schaeffer concluded that these could only be the result of great catastrophes.[8]

2. The strange world of the ancients differed in several ways from our own. This fact does not necessarily imply catastrophes. But a simple extrapolation of present rates and conditions back to ancient times does not account for the differences; it suggests an abrupt alteration from outside forces. Consider two examples. First is the striking evidence that the pole star seen by the Egyptians in the nineteenth century B.C. was not Polaris but a star in the Great Bear constellation (popularly called the Big Dipper).[9] This is in major contradiction with the extrapolation of Earth's current axial precession rate which calculates the pole star of the ancients to be very much nearer to Polaris. A second example is archaeological evidence that the downfall of civilizations (mentioned above) was concurrent with abrupt "climatic changes which seem to have brought about transformation in the occupation and the economy of the country."[10] Slow climatic changes are known to occur (and still are occurring), but a widespread abrupt change suggests an unusual cause, probably extraterrestrial.

3. Flood traditions were a part of the folklores of many cultures. This is perhaps the most striking thing to be observed in surveying these ancient traditions. A geographer of the last century named Andree claimed to have compiled Flood traditions of eighty-eight different cultures and societies, equally distributed between the eastern and western hemispheres. Many details differ between these myths but a very strong common theme emerges: several people are saved on a boat from a worldwide Flood. A summary of Flood traditions is given in a book by Alfred M. Rehwinkel.[11]

4. The ancients were preoccupied with the astral. In the ancient world, following the stars and other celestial bodies was not simply recreation, it seemed to permeate every part of life. Architectural structures were designed to trace by shadow the path of the sun. The obelisk, ziggurat, sundial, and similar structures found in both hemispheres were designed for this purpose.[12] Furthermore, the ancient religions generally involved the worship of heavenly bodies.

8. Quoted in *Bombarded Earth*, pp. 214, 215.

9. *Bombarded Earth*, pp. 146-148; *Worlds in Collision*, pp. 313, 314.

10. *Bombarded Earth*, pp. 214, 215, quoting C. F. A. Schaeffer.

11. *The Flood* (St. Louis: Concordia, 1951), pp. 127-176. See also Arthur C. Custance, "Flood Traditions of the World," in *Symposium on Creation IV*, ed. Donald W. Patten (Grand Rapids: Baker, 1972), pp. 9-43.

12. *Worlds in Collision*, pp. 317-323.

The Jewish historian Josephus described the patriarch Abraham as being *alone* in his belief that one should worship the Creator rather than the heavenly bodies themselves.[13] The ancients were pre-occupied with the astral for a reason; great upheavals on Earth had been accompanied by great irregularities in the heavens. Hence they tracked celestial bodies with great concern and apprehension in anticipation of further disturbances.

5. Calendaric changes were necessary in ancient times. The Egyptians are known to have introduced more than one change in the length of their years.[14] Velikovsky has assembled evidence that other peoples of the ancient world made similar changes.[15] Only a massive extraterrestrial force could produce such an abrupt change.

6. Details of specific catastrophes pictured in ancient literature and mythology are utterly frightening: darkness, earthquakes, falling fire, falling stones, massive simultaneous vulcanism, noise and tumult, lightning and strong winds.[16] All of these occur today on a local scale with limited intensity, but the frightening accounts of the ancients go far beyond this. Some of these upheavals are likely of extraterrestrial origin (falling stones, fire) and others strongly suggest extraterrestrial causes (massive vulcanism, widespread earthquakes).

There are other ancient reports of cataclysms in the heavens not directly affecting Earth: for example, the mysterious disappearance of the planet Electra.[17] But the pattern has been established: the ancients report a number of great catastrophes which severely affect man and his environment.

Physical records: disturbance and discontinuity. A careful observer of Earth's great physical wonders is certain to be impressed by the scale and beauty of such spectacles. Many of these great wonders testify of birth by trauma and many exhibit the scars of harrowing destruction. Indeed, evidence comes from every quarter that the history of Earth's crust is one of trauma and cataclysm. Geologists have assembled a great volume of facts supporting global catastrophism. This is in spite of the domination of their science by the unifor-

13. *The Antiquities of the Jews,* trans. William Whiston (Bridgeport, Conn.: M. Sherman, 1828), pp. 94, 95.

14. *Bombarded Earth,* pp. 212, 213.

15. *Worlds in Collision,* pp. 330-359.

16. Ibid., pp. 53-65, 91-93.

17. Donald W. Patten, *The Biblical Flood and the Ice Epoch* (Seattle: Pacific Meridian, 1966), pp. 45, 46.

mitarian axiom of a peaceful Earth history. It is feasible only to summarize the results of this research.[18]

1. Sediments compose the majority of Earth's exposed crust. Sedimentary rock is laid in strata by waters bearing soil or minerals. According to uniformitarian assumption, these layers were deposited for ages at the same minute rate as today. In an article on stratigraphy (the study of sediments), Stuart E. Nevins cites several reasons why the sedimentary record could not have been laid in the leisurely manner that sediments are presently being formed. First, several types of sedimentary rock are formed only by violently rushing or turbulent water. Second, some kinds of sediment are *not* being formed today, which contradicts an axiom of uniformitarianism. Many coal deposits could not have been formed by peaceful sedimentation in a swamp (a popular uniformitarian theory); the topsy-turvy orientation of trees and other fossils in them reflects violent formation. Finally, these sedimentary layers seem to follow global patterns. This is not yet a firm conclusion but preliminary work seems to support it. If it is true, then one may conclude that the sedimentation was global as well as catastrophic.[19]

2. Mass extinction of life forms is apparent in the sediments. If one peers closely into the strata, he will find that the solid rock is actually a tomb for countless myriads of fossils—animal and plant, large and small. The basic requirement for the preservation of a fossil is a burial more rapid than the decay time of the carcass.[20] This is not the kind of burial a creature would receive at the current sedimentation rate; the burial of a medium sized shellfish may take hundreds of years. In addition to being rapid, the burial of fossils seems to have been both worldwide and simultaneous. This realization led a paleontologist to write, "The worldwide incidence of extinction . . . leads one to look for an extraterrestrial cosmic cause."[21] Similar extinctions have been caused by the massive onset of ice, burying flora and fauna of diverse types in the higher latitudes. In many places the ice remains until today, and many of these specimens can

18. Most geologists are uniformitarians, and many have tried strenuously to force a uniformitarian interpretation on the facts of the physical record. This author intends to interpret the facts in this section in the simplest and most natural way.

19. "Stratigraphic Evidence of the Flood," in *Symposium on Creation III*, ed. Donald W. Patten (Grand Rapids: Baker, 1971), pp. 32-65. Under certain flooding conditions, sediments may be laid at a significantly higher rate than the average global rate. But the picture presented in the sedimentary record seems to indicate widespread—even global—sedimentation that took place more or less simultaneously. This violates substantive uniformitarianism, which permits only local deviations from the global mean rate of sedimentation (which is taken as constant in time).

20. Clifford L. Burdick, "The Structure and Fabric of Geology," *Creation Research Society Quarterly* 7 (December 1970): 144, 145.

21. *Bombarded Earth*, p. 115, quoting H. Linger.

108   LOREN C. STEINHAUER

be found perfectly preserved in the polar deep freeze. The manner of extinction seems to have been violent as well as rapid. In both cases (fossilized and frozen) many of the creatures were torn and broken as they died. These extinctions involved incredible numbers of animals. The creatures were packed together and buried in numbers that boggle the imagination. In other places where fossilization or freezing did not occur, one can find bone graveyards in which literally millions of bones of diverse animals are all mixed together. Indeed, mass extinction is one of the strongest physical evidences for global catastrophism.[22]

3. Meteoric bombardment has left a number of craters on Earth, some of which were once thought volcanic in origin. Gallant lists a number of known meteor craters and others that are possibly such.[23] Some of these are many miles in diameter. Such an impact would certainly generate a major local disturbance, if not a global upheaval due to the generation of tidal waves or earthquakes.

4. Massive glaciation has left clear marks in large areas in both the northern and southern hemispheres. There has long been the theory of repeated ice ages, but another theory is that physical evidence supports a single great ice epoch.[24] It was rapid in onset, as testified by the sudden burial and freezing of many life forms. It seems that only an extraterrestrial cause could produce such a sudden onset of a glacial epoch.[25]

5. The unusual world of the past is reflected in the physical record. The outstanding difference between our world and that of the ancients may be the great difference in climate: moistness in today's deserts, temperate and even subtropical vegetation in today's polar regions.[26] Furthermore, there is paleomagnetic evidence that Earth's magnetic field has experienced reversals (at least locally) in polarity.[27] Of course vastly different conditions in the past do not necessarily imply rapid change, but these are seemingly unaccountable by an extrapolation of present conditions.

22. Two interesting articles on recently discovered frozen mammoths have appeared in the popular press: Ivan T. Sanderson, "Riddle of the Quick-Frozen Giants," *Saturday Evening Post* 232 (January 16, 1960): 39ff.; Charles H. Hapgood, "The Mystery of the Frozen Mammoths," *Coronet* 48 (September 1960): 71ff.

23. *Bombarded Earth*, part 2: chapters 1 and 2.

24. William A. Springstead, "Monoglaciology and the Global Flood," *Creation Research Society Quarterly* 8 (December 1971): 175-82. Uniformitarians have been able to accommodate the concept of ice ages by assuming that they appeared slowly, during periods spanning thousands of years, but the frozen mammoths and the evidence assembled by Springstead indicate that the ice age(s) had a rapid onset.

25. *The Biblical Flood*, pp. 101-136.

26. Dolph E. Hooker, *Those Astounding Ice Ages* (New York: Exposition, 1958).

27. Allan Cox, G. Brent Dalrymple, and Richard R. Doell, "Reversals in Earth's Magnetic Field," *Scientific American* 216 (February 1967): 44-54.

6. Extraterrestrial catastrophes have left their mark on the solar system. Among them are the rings of Saturn and the asteroids, which appear to be the irregular fragments of a body pulled apart by gravitational forces.[28] Also, there are huge craters on the moon and Mars (many, if not most, of which are meteoric in origin). This shows that there have been *major* collisions of meteors with bodies near the Earth, which renders plausible the suggestion that Earth has experienced the same.

It is then a firm conclusion from physical evidence that Earth has experienced violent catastrophes in the past, some of which were global in scope and extraterrestrial in cause. Moreover, the testimony of all three witnesses displays obvious correlations, which is what we should see if the testimony is true. The overall conclusion is that, while there were long peaceful periods in ancient times, allowing great civilizations to develop, there were also a few violent global catastrophes. This thesis is so heavily supported by evidence that it may even be described as obviously true. In the area of Earth history, science has been stifled by false presuppositions for 150 years. Uniformitarian presuppositions have hidden the obvious and championed the incredible. Science must be rid of them.

28. Neither the catastrophic origin of the asteroids nor the meteoric origin of lunar and Martian craters has been established firmly, but certain facts seem to support these conclusions: for example, the asteroids are irregular, seemingly broken fragments, suggesting a catastrophic origin; and lunar craters and terrestrial meteor craters are very similar, suggesting a meteoric origin for lunar craters.

7

Gregor Mendel

Bolton Davidheiser

Gregor Mendel, as is well known, founded the science of genetics. What is less well known is that his experiments duplicated (about one hundred years later) those of Pierre Maupertuis,[1] of whom Mendel was ignorant, and were in turn duplicated by Hugo De Vries, who was then ignorant of Mendel.

Mendel and Maupertuis form an interesting contrast. Mendel was religious, a monk who became the abbot of his monastery, and Maupertuis was irreligious. Maupertuis, by training a physical scientist, took up biology to refute the argument that nature furnishes decisive evidence for the existence of God. Mendel's work was virtually ignored by the scientific community of his time, but he has been given his due in the twentieth century. Maupertuis, on the other hand, enjoyed great fame until Voltaire took sides against him in a quarrel and ruined his reputation; today he is virtually unknown. The apostle Paul affirms in Romans 1 that the idolatrous heathen, because of the evidence in nature of the creative acts of God, are without excuse. How much more, then, is a genius like Maupertuis, not to mention scientists of our day—all of whom know far more than the heathen of Paul's day—without excuse.

Mendel's Life

Mendel was born of peasant parentage, July 22 (or 20), 1822, in a village located in what is now Czechoslovakia. His given name was Johann, and he took the name of Gregor when he entered the monastery. The family name, Mendel, is probably a corruption of Emmanuel, a Jewish name meaning "God with us," but there is no

1. Bentley Glass, ed., *Forerunners of Darwin: 1745-1859* (Baltimore: Johns Hopkins, 1969), pp. 57, 60, 74.

111

evidence that Johann Mendel had any Jewish ancestry; in fact, his earliest recorded ancestors were Protestants. For this reason there also are other theories as to the origin of his family name.

Johann had two sisters; one was physically and temperamentally like the father and the other like the mother. Johann, interestingly enough, was more of a "hybrid."

He was such an outstanding student in the local school that the teacher urged his parents to allow him to continue his education. This was unusual for a peasant, but with his father's consent the eleven-year-old youth went to a school thirteen miles from home. A note in the margin of the records describes him as the top student of his class. From there he went to another school, this one twenty miles from home. Here, because of financial difficulties, he was on "half rations." Sometimes his family sent him bread and butter, but he never had enough. In spite of this he was graded "super excellent" in nearly all his studies, but because of this his health failed, as it had once before. When his father was permanently injured—a log accidentally crushed his chest—Johann's education seemed to be at an end. But his older sister had married and the Mendel farm was turned over to her husband; and the younger sister gave Johann a part of her dowry. So he continued his studies, tutoring on the side. The strain was too much, however, and his health failed for the third time.

He was given the opportunity to enter a monastery and he did, as he explained in his autobiography, not because he felt called there but because of financial considerations. The monastery was a cultural center and gave him the opportunity to pursue his studies.

Shortly after entering the monastery at the age of twenty-five and before he had completed his training, he was ordained a priest, primarily because there was a shortage of priests. While fulfilling his preparation, he was reprimanded for not wearing a cap, something required of all students.

Visiting the sick made him so violently ill that he had to be relieved of this pastoral duty. He became a "supply teacher" but failed the test which would have given him status as a permanent teacher. For more studies he went to the university at Vienna. There he received evolutionary teaching, although he left the university six years before the publication of Darwin's *Origin of Species*. One of his professors, Franz Unger, taught that the plant and animal world "had gradually developed itself step by step."[2] Some members of the faculty called Unger a corrupter of youth and said he should be expelled; three years after Mendel left the university, Unger resigned. Mendel then took the test once more to become an accredited teacher, and again he failed. One story has it that he became ill and

2. *Botanical Letters to a Friend*, trans. B. Paul (London, 1853), p. 107.

did not finish, another that he had a dispute with one of the examiners about a question in botany. At any rate he never tried again and remained a supply teacher all the fourteen years of his teaching career. It is certain he was an excellent teacher. He had a good knowledge of the subject matter and made the work so interesting that the students looked forward to class.

He began his famous hybridizing experiments shortly after failing the accrediting test for the second time, May 5, 1856, and it has been suggested that his work was a result of the argument he had with one of the examiners. But he had planned the experiments long before this; before beginning them, he carefully grew his peas for two seasons to make sure he had pure stocks.

Furthermore, Mendel crossed gray and white mice in his room, and Iltis suggests that Mendel carried on this work *before* his plant hybridization experiments. Mendel never mentioned the mouse work in writing. Some contemporaries questioned the propriety of a priest studying natural history, and some of Mendel's constituency would have been shocked to know that he was breeding mice. So he gave it up for plant breeding.

It has been pointed out, as we shall see, that when Mendel did his plant work he seemed to know what ratios to expect. Perhaps he already had worked this out with the mice and did the plant work in order to obtain data which he could feel free to publish. But on the other hand, if he obtained several 3:1 ratios from crossing peas, it is not surprising that he thereafter should have expected them.

Mendel's own words relating to the undertaking of his experiments are: "Artificial fertilizations undertaken in ornamental plants in order to produce new color varieties were the occasion of the experiments here described. The remarkable regularity with which the same hybrid forms continually recurred when the fertilization took place between like species led me to undertake further experiments designed to follow up the development of the hybrids in their offspring."[3]

In 1868 it became necessary to elect a new abbot for the monastery, and the choice fell upon Gregor Mendel. It has sometimes been said that he did not desire the position and having it thrust upon him was a great surprise. That such is not the case is clear in a letter he wrote March 26, 1868, a few days before the election. But shortly after his election he wrote to Karl Wilhelm Nägeli that it was "altogether unexpected."[4]

As the new abbot, Mendel had to give up his teaching, which he enjoyed so much and did so well in spite of twice being rejected as incompetent by the examiners in Vienna. He gave his last month's

3. "Experiments with Plant Hybrids," 1866.

4. Hugo Iltis, *Life of Mendel* (New York: Hafner, 1966), pp. 239, 240.

salary to the students. He believed his new office would afford him time to continue his researches, but many duties related to it, as well as to positions he held in various societies and businesses, took up his time.

Politically Mendel was a "pronounced liberal." Because of this it was especially mortifying to him when the Liberal Party caused the dispute that occupied and vexed the final decade of his life. The party passed a law levying a tax on religious communities "in order to supply the financial needs of Catholic worship." Mendel, who, when he became abbot, pledged himself to protect the property of the monastery, declared the tax unconstitutional and refused to pay it. When he made the required financial report, he did not even mention the allowable deductions. He sent some money from his personal funds, making it clear that this was a voluntary contribution and not a payment of the tax. It was returned and the original demand was repeated. He then made the first in a long series of protests. In return the government began impounding rents due the monastery. Mendel retaliated by charging the government five percent interest upon these accounts, to be paid when the money should be returned.

Mendel was a very prominent person by this time and was performing valuable services for the government. The situation became embarrassing and to save face the government was willing to accept a token payment, but Mendel considered it a matter of principle and was adamant. He was bribed by talk of being offered the Order of Leopold, but to no avail. He was threatened by talk of being deprived of some of his public offices, once again to no avail.

The other tragedy in the life of Mendel was his seven-year correspondence with Nägeli, a Swiss botanist. Nägeli was one of the chief plant hybridizers of the day, but instead of taking an interest in Mendel's work, he snubbed him. Either he did not take the trouble to understand what Mendel was doing or he did not read carefully what Mendel was telling him. There is little doubt that he was influenced by the fact that Mendel's results were not in accord with his own theories and conclusions. He suggested that Mendel begin hybridizing hawkweeds (*Hieracium*), and Mendel unfortunately took this advice. Besides the technical difficulties of working with such small individual flowers in the inflorescence, there was the fact unknown to Nägeli and Mendel that hawkweeds set seed without fertilization. Thus the product of much labor was figuratively fruitless. Actually it was worse than fruitless, because crosses appeared to have been made which had not, and the results appeared to deny the validity of Mendel's work with the peas.

Mendel grew very corpulent and smoked as many as twenty cigars a day. He suffered from heart disease and kidney trouble. Finally he had to be relieved of his duties as abbot, and one Ambrose Poje was elected to succeed him. Mendel died, January 6, 1884. His notebooks and papers were burned; only his well-bound books were spared. The new abbot promptly negotiated the tax with the government. In the end, due to deductions and overpayments by way of the impounded rents, the monastery was given a refund and exempted from taxation for the remainder of the decade.

Mendel's Discoveries

Not until the close of the seventeenth century had sexual reproduction been demonstrated in plants. In 1694 Camerarius, a physician in Tübingen, concluded from his experiments that pollen functions as the male element and ovules as the female. The most famous name in plant hybridization before Mendel was Joseph Gottlieb Kölreuter, who in 1760 performed the first careful experiments in the area; he crossed two species of tobacco by placing the pollen of one upon the stigmas of the other.

Between the works of Kölreuter and Mendel, hybridizers found that in general plant hybrids tend to inherit about equally from each parent type, producing a condition which is an average of that of the parents. It was found that in some progenies individuals might be more like one or the other parent type.

Charles Darwin himself did quite a bit of plant hybridizing. For the most part this resulted only in a multitude of tedious measurements of flower parts with very little scientific significance. But working with the snapdragon *Antirrhinum majus*, he crossed the common irregular variety with the peloric, which has a regular corolla. He made the cross both ways and found that the hybrids were all of the common variety. But when these were allowed to self-fertilize, he observed in the second generation 88 plants which had the common type of flowers and 37 which had peloric (plus two which were abnormal).[5] This is a good 3:1 ratio, with a chi-square of 1.41. If the experiment were repeated a number of times, one would expect to get a result this far or further from 3:1 nearly 30 percent of the time. These results, however, meant nothing to Darwin.

It must be remembered that Mendel did his work before chromosomes were known; not until his work was rediscovered did evidence accumulate that the hereditary factors are on the chromosomes. Although Darwin had noticed cases where a characteristic may skip a generation (recessiveness), it was left to Mendel to see that this

5. *The Variation of Animals and Plants Under Domestication*, 2 vols. (London: D. Appleton, 1896),2:46. It is reported that Darwin got some essentially perfect 3:1 ratios in the second generation of crosses between short style (dominant) and long style in *Primula auriculata*. Peter R. Bell, *Darwin's Biological Work* (New York: Cambridge University, 1959), p. 241.

means the factors for these characteristics are in pairs, a member of each pair being supplied by each parent. It follows from this that the reproductive cells (gametes) must have just one member of the pair (must be haploid). In a pure strain (homozygous) the two members of a pair of factors will be the same, while in a hybrid (heterozygous) they will be different (alleles).

When a hybrid forms reproductive cells, it follows that only one member of the pair of factors can go into one reproductive cell, so there will be a *segregation* of factors. This is Mendel's first law, the law of segregation: *In the formation of the reproductive cells, or gametes, genes of a pair (alleles) segregate* (fig. 1).

When an animal or plant is hybrid for more than one pair of factors, then the factors of different pairs assort at random in the formation of gametes. This is Mendel's second law, the law of independent assortment: *In the formation of the gametes, genes which are not alleles assort at random* (fig. 2).

Some authors write of a "law of dominance," but there really is no such thing. In the seven pairs of alleles used by Mendel in his peas, one member of each pair was dominant. There are many cases in which there is a lack of dominance and the hybrids usually are a blend of the parental types. Also there are cases where a gene acts as though dominant over another gene which is not its allele. This is called *epistasis*. The genes, however, are inherited exactly the same way whether there is dominance or not.

As a consequence of Mendel's two laws, fertilization produces the

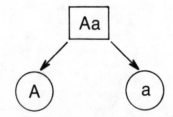

Fig. 1. The law of segregation

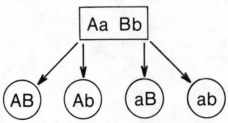

Fig. 2. The law of independent assortment

famous 3:1 and 9:3:3:1 ratios in monohybrid and dihybrid crosses when there is dominance. Of course the same genotypes are produced, with different phenotypic expression, in cases of lack of dominance and epistasis. See figure 3.

P_1	AA	x	aa
Gametes	A		a
F_1		Aa	

Gametes		A	a
	A	AA	Aa
F_2	a	Aa	aa

3 A- : 1 aa

P_1	AABB	x	aabb	or	(AAbb	x	aaBB)
Gametes	AB		ab		(Ab		aB)
F_1		AaBb					

Gametes		AB	Ab	aB	ab
	AB	AABB	AABb	AaBB	AaBb
	Ab	AABb	AAbb	AaBb	Aabb
F_2	aB	AaBB	AaBb	aaBB	aaBb
	ab	AaBb	Aabb	aaBb	aabb

9 A-B- : 3 A-bb : 3 aaB- : 1 aabb

Fig. 3. The 3:1 (above) and 9:3:3:1 (below) ratios

Mendel's laws of inheritance were an important discovery, but of course inheritance is not this simple. If it were, students could learn it in a lesson or two and there would be no courses in advanced genetics. It is said that Mendel tested 34 varieties of peas and selected 21 for experiments. In his genetic studies he worked with seven pairs of contrasting characteristics and, unknown to him, peas have seven pairs of chromosomes. By a strange coincidence (we assume), each of the pairs of genes he used was on a different chromosome. But if he had used just one more pair of genes, that pair by necessity would have had to be on the same chromosome as one of the other pairs. Then if he had made all the possible kinds of crosses using his pairs of genes two at a time, he would have been surprised; his second law would not have always applied. There would not be independent assortment in all cases. Genes on the same chromosome would be "linked." But because of the phenomenon of crossing-over, there would be exceptions to this exception and such genes would not always be linked. (This was called "coupling and repulsion" before the phenomenon was understood.) Sex-linked and sex-limited inheritance are other types of exceptions to Mendel's laws, and there are many more. But there is nothing mysterious about any of them, and Mendel's laws are basic.

When Mendel tabulated the numbers of the different characteristics represented by his peas, he got very good ratios. In fact, his ratios were too good. It is evident that he knew what the ratios should be and, consciously or unconsciously, this influenced his tabulating. R. A. Fisher seems to assume deliberate falsification,[6] while Sewall Wright points out difficulties involved in this kind of counting which should be taken into consideration.[7] The grand total in the second hybrid generation for Mendel's seven pairs of contrasting characteristics in the pea were: dominants 14,949 and recessives 5,010. The chi-square is only .107, and with one degree of freedom, a result this far or further from the expected 3:1 ratio should occur more than 70 percent of the time. Fisher says that a discrepancy of "so low a value could scarcely occur once in 2,000 trials. There can be no doubt that the data from later years of the experiment have been biased strongly in the direction of agreement with expectations." Fisher cites an interesting instance when Mendel was expecting a 2:1 ratio. The correct ratio in this case was 1.8874 : 1.1126, but Mendel's recorded count, which was very close to 2:1, was sufficiently far from the correct ratio that it could be expected only once in twenty-nine trials.[8]

6. "Has Mendel's Work Been Rediscovered?" in *The Origin of Genetics,* ed. Curt Stern and Eva Sherwood (San Francisco: W. H. Freeman, 1966), p. 168.

7. In *The Origin of Genetics.*

8. "Mendel's Work."

There are several reasons why Mendel succeeded while others before him failed. In the first place he started with pure stock, having grown his peas for two seasons before making any crosses; he could tell if the characteristics did not breed true. He worked with contrasting pairs of simple, clear-cut, easily observed characteristics. He kept a count of the numbers of every type that resulted from his crosses, enabling him to find the ratio which was the clue to inheritance.

Mendel and Evolution

There remains the perplexing question of why Mendel's work was so long neglected. The reason once given most frequently was that the journal of the Brünn Society for the Study of Natural Science, of which Mendel was a member, was so obscure that Mendel did not come to the attention of scientists. This was not the case. The journal was sent to 120 libraries, including eleven in the United States. Mendel's papers were listed in various bibliographies. He corresponded extensively with Nägeli, a prominent plant hybridizer, and his name was even mentioned at the end of the article "Hybridism" in the ninth edition of the *Encyclopaedia Britannica* (1878).

Another reason given is the *Zeitgeist,* or the "spirit of the times." It is said that the scientists of Mendel's day were interested in other matters, such as classification, and not in hybridizing. But Charles Darwin was doing a great deal of hybridizing which, though of little value, was considered quite important, and Nägeli also was well known for his extensive hybridizing experiments.

A reason which has been promoted of late is that the biological scientists were unaccustomed to a "mathematical" approach and could not understand Mendel. This seems a very weak excuse. Mendel did not get so mathematically involved that he statistically analyzed his observed ratios; his ratios were too good to need statistical analysis.

The fourth reason is that Mendel's findings challenged contemporary views, especially evolutionary ones. Mendel himself said, "I know that the results I obtained were not easily compatible with our contemporary scientific knowledge, and that under the circumstances publication of one such isolated experiment was doubly dangerous; dangerous for experimenter and for the cause he represented."[9]

William Bateson suggested that Mendel undertook his hybridization experiments to discredit Darwin's views.[10] But Mendel began

9. *Letter to Karl Wilhelm Nägeli,* April 18, 1867. Quoted in *Mendel Centenary: Genetics, Development and Evolution,* ed. Roland N. Nardone (Washington, D.C.: Catholic University of America, 1966), p. 168.

10. *Mendel's Principles of Heredity* (New York: Cambridge University, 1909), p. 311.

his work several years before Darwin published *Origin of Species*, and before the book appeared only a few of Darwin's intimate associates knew about his evolutionary views. By the time Mendel published his paper, however, he no doubt knew of Darwin's work, as Fisher has suggested.[11] Fisher also points out that Mendel referred in his paper to a well-known plant breeder's opinion that the data opposed the theory of evolution, and Mendel took issue with that opinion.[12] After Mendel read the first part of his now-famous paper, "Experiments with Plant Hybrids," to the Brünn Society, writes Harry Sootin, "The remainder of that historic evening in Brünn was devoted to other business, including an exciting discussion of certain aspects of Darwinism." Sootin does not divulge the source of his information.[13]

The evidence points to the conclusion that Mendel, influenced by Unger, his former professor, began his hybridization experiments to gather evidence concerning the theory of evolution. He knew nothing of Darwin's evolutionary views when he began, but was well acquainted with them years later: Hugo Iltis writes that Darwin's publications were interesting and stimulating to Mendel, and that one of them in the monastery library contained numerous notations in Mendel's handwriting.[14] Mendel recognized the bearing of the mechanism of heredity upon evolutionary theory. He prefaced his famous paper, published in 1866, with these words: "It requires indeed some courage to undertake a labor of such far-reaching extent; this appears, however, to be the only right way by which we can finally reach the solution of a question the importance of which cannot be overestimated in connection with the history of the evolution of organic forms." Bateson's opinion notwithstanding, Mendel appears to have accepted the theory of evolution.

Be this as it may, it is evident that Mendel's results are contrary to Darwin's pangenesis theory, and furthermore they do not fit Darwin's idea of natural selection. According to Darwin, small variations are constantly occurring in a population and the better have survival value. This is quite different from the stable Mendelian characteristics which can skip one or more generations but reappear exactly the same as they were before. Since Darwinism was held in such high esteem by influential persons, it is not at all surprising that Mendel's work should be opposed on this ground.

At the turn of the century, Mendel's work was repeated and rediscovered by De Vries in Holland and Correns in Germany. The name of von Tschermak in Austria generally is associated with this

11. "Mendel's Work," pp. 143, 144.

12. Ibid., p. 168.

13. *Gregor Mendel* (New York: Vanguard, 1959), p. 180.

14. *Life of Mendel*, p. 104.

also, but he did not analyze his data or interpret it; he worked with yellow and green seeds in peas, and his results were even closer to the 3:1 ratio than were Mendel's.

At approximately the same time that Mendel's laws were rediscovered, Wilhelm Johannsen published his classic paper, "Heredity in Populations and Pure Lines."[15] The translator of the paper says of it: "This thorough and meticulous investigation of the true significance of selection was a bombshell to evolutionary thought. The efficacy of selection in the production of new species had been one of the mainstays of Darwin's theory of evolution. Johannsen's studies demonstrated conclusively that selection could not extend the limits of previously established variability."[16] It was also at this time that De Vries proposed the mutation theory as the answer to the problem of the origin of evolutionary difference. These developments caused a reaction against Darwinism as the method of evolution, but before long this attitude changed and the new concepts were incorporated with Darwin's natural selection theory. The modern synthetic theory of evolution was being born.

A generation later, evolutionists again were saying that all of this was an inadequate explanation of evolution, and they promised that, given time, they would come up with an adequate one. A great deal of research has been done since that time and the ultimate material of the genetic code has been probed. There is talk of performing "genetic surgery" to alter the genetic code to specifications determined by the scientists. But they have found no better explanation of evolution than natural selection and mutations (plus such things as hybridization, polyploidy, and genetic drift); therefore a number of recent evolutionists have said that evolution is firmly established on the basis of natural selection and mutations.

However, there are more flies in the ointment. The rather recently discovered "neutral mutations," which should not show the effect of selection but do, and research done on newly-developed, high-speed computers, are again casting doubts in the minds of some. Where these developments will lead remains to be seen. Unfortunately one thing is certain: most evolutionists will not be moved by evidence that has accumulated against their theory—their evolutionary outlook is more like a religion than science. They will not be moved by the evidence in nature of the acts of God, preferring the evolutionary theory which substitutes natural laws for divine creation.

Christians will continue to recognize the handiwork of God in nature and to glorify Him for His creation.

15. Reprinted in *Classic Papers in Genetics*, ed. James A. Peters (New York: Prentice-Hall, 1959), pp. 20-26.
16. Ibid., p. 20.

"Hearken unto this, O Job: stand still, and consider the wondrous works of God" (Job 37:14).

"Who is this that darkeneth counsel by words without knowledge?" (Job 38:2).

8

Genetics and Jacob's Flock

W. Dennis Burrowes

The Bible was not designed as a science textbook; it employs neither the forms of thought nor the nomenclature of science. Many of its statements do, however, have historical and scientific implications which, if they are not accurate, reflect upon the origin of Scripture. If it is inspired by the Creator of all nature, it must be completely reliable. God may not have intended Scripture to be a scientific text, but certainly He did not intend it to teach scientific error! If, on the other hand, the Bible were a merely human composition, it could be expected to contain errors, and scientific errors could be expected especially in the earliest books such as the Pentateuch and Job. We are not referring to Scripture's description of Creation; that has been dealt with extensively by creationist writers and falls outside the scope of experimental science. We refer instead to such accounts as the one in Genesis 30:25-31:16—Jacob's livestock breeding. This involves principles of genetics, a relatively new science even in our day.

The Account in Genesis

Jacob was a "supplanter," a schemer from birth. He was born clutching the heel of his twin brother Esau and for this reason was named Jacob, meaning "heel-holder." But even *before* his birth, God revealed that he should be the father of a great nation and that he should have the ascendancy over his senior twin.

As Jacob grew up, he genuinely desired the blessing of God, but he was crooked by nature, trying to secure the best by deceit and trickery. He supplanted his elder brother by taking first his birthright and then the blessing of the aging Isaac, their father. As a result he had to flee for his life from Palestine to Padan-aram (Padan in Mesopotamia), the ancestral home town. There Jacob met his maternal uncle Laban, a ruthless bargainer and Jacob's equal in craftiness. Jacob served him seven years for the hand of his daughter Rachel, whom he loved; at the end of that period, Laban deceitfully gave him his elder daughter Leah instead. So Jacob served another seven years for Rachel. These two wives and their two handmaids bore eleven sons and one daughter during Jacob's sojourn in Padan-aram.

When Jacob wanted to return to his own country, he asked to be released along with his wives and children. Laban, who spoke the truth this time, replied that God had blessed him for Jacob's sake. He proposed to Jacob that he should name his own wages and remain with Laban. With characteristic subtlety Jacob said that he wanted no wages; he only wanted to take from Laban's flock the minority of lambs or sheep that were brown, black, speckled, or spotted, and any goats that were speckled or spotted. Jacob underscored the righteousness of his intentions by pronouncing that Laban should be free to deal with him as a thief if he were to find any animals of the standard color among Jacob's flock. Jacob "generously" proposed to undertake the separation of the flocks himself, and to do it immediately.

Equally "accommodating," Laban consented willingly but then, that same day, personally removed from the flocks all the male goats that were ringstraked (striped) or spotted, and all the female goats that were speckled or spotted. The account indicates that he made sure to remove every goat which "had any white in it" that his eye could detect, including some ringstraked (striped) he-goats, which Jacob had not specifically mentioned. Laban also removed the black or brown lambs. The account does not say he removed the "speckled and spotted" sheep mentioned by Jacob, possibly because they were extremely rare among Laban's sheep—or even absent altogether. Then Laban gave all these off-colored animals to his son and separated himself and his flock by the very safe distance of three days' journey from the flocks which Jacob continued to tend. By this means Laban insured that, at the start of the proposed arrangement, Jacob's flock contained not one of these color classes (phenotypes)[1] which were to be his wages and possession.

Once again Laban's craftiness had anticipated Jacob's, who evidently made no complaint at this stage; for although Laban was cheating in the moral sense, he had the legal right to do as he pleased

---

1. *Phenotype* is the visible characteristics of an organism, as opposed to *genotype*, which is an organism's genetic constitution and includes dominant (expressed) and recessive (unexpressed, dormant) characteristics.

with his own herd. True to nature, Jacob silently resorted to counter-strategy.

Jacob had acquired certain notions, probably current at the time, about prenatal influence, or maternal impression. He thought that by placing varicolored objects before mating animals, the ewes and she-goats would produce varicolored kids and lambs. Jacob probably knew by experience that off-colored animals would eventually reappear in Laban's flock, but this would take too long. So Jacob collected branches of three kinds of trees which, when partially stripped, would show a color contrast between the bark and the underlying cambium. He peeled strips off these branches and laid them in the watering troughs. As every observer knows, this quiet interlude is when mating often occurs during the breeding season. About five months later, behold! The flocks brought forth some striped, speckled, and spotted kids. Genesis 30:39 focuses attention on the varicolored effects of Jacob's strategy; this is probably why it does not specifically mention brown lambs, although verse 40 shows that some brown lambs were in fact born.

To further intensify the supposed influence of varicolored objects, Jacob divided the flocks and set the striped goats and the brown lambs before the eyes of the breeding animals. So he built up his herd of varicolored animals, keeping them separate from Laban's own flock.

Jacob took his scheme one step further to insure that his flock included no second-class animals—Laban could have these! The early spring lambs, conceived in the previous autumn, were generally superior to the autumn lambs, conceived in the previous spring; so Jacob used the peeled rods only with the "stronger" sheep. The Hebrew words translated "strong" and "feeble" are evidently technical terms. Several ancient interpreters, who probably were well acquainted with these terms, agree that they mean "early" and "late" lambs or kids. This would explain why the strong and feeble animals mated at distinct times, as the narrative implies: they belonged to distinct age-groups. The word translated "cattle" could be used of goats as well as sheep, so this technique was probably applied to both. Jacob's plan worked admirably, and he became very wealthy at Laban's expense.

The story is a good one, full of human interest and realistic detail, but there is one snag: there is no scientific evidence that the color of animals can be controlled by the prenatal environment of the dam! Coat color is inherited in accord with established laws of heredity, and neither experimental observation nor theoretical considerations have confirmed any *corresponding* influence of the environment, whereby spotted objects induce spotted offspring. This is a popular notion, however, accepted by many of the old and even

some of the newer Bible commentators on this passage.[2] It could
easily survive among herdsmen since the desired color will occasionally appear by normal hereditary processes.

To return to the narrative, Jacob's prosperity increased and, after
several years, Laban became distinctly hostile toward him. Jacob
sensed his change of attitude. About this time Jehovah appeared to
Jacob and told him to return to the land of his fathers. Jacob called
his two wives and told them of Jehovah's command, as well as of a
dream. In this dream God showed Jacob a picture of "striped,
spotted and piebald" sires leaping upon the flocks. The vision occurred at breeding season when Jacob's mind would naturally have
been occupied with the success of his scheme. God said, "For I have
seen all that Laban doeth unto thee," and impressed upon Jacob that
the growth of his herd was a direct consequence of divine intervention; God had taken care of Jacob because He was the "God of
Bethel, where thou anointedst the pillar, and where thou vowedst a
vow unto me." Besides blessing Jacob, Jehovah was also judging
Laban.

But, once again the pattern of Jacob's life was repeated. He
desired blessing and schemed to get it. God blessed him in spite of,
not because of, his schemes; He also allowed him to experience the
evil consequences of his carnal methods—the hatred of his victims.
How painful it is for clever people to learn to depend upon God.
This spiritual lesson is the primary point of this narrative, but the
facts recorded to establish this lesson incidentally provide a lesson in
the principles of heredity, designed and established by the Creator
Himself.

Jacob's dream revealed that the production of off-colored lambs
and kids had occurred through the genetic transmission and segregation of inherited characteristics, a process which wasn't explained until 3,500 years later by Gregor Mendel and Hugo De Vries.
The striped, speckled, and spotted patterns were due not to the
environmental influence of Jacob's peeled rods but to the genetic
influence of striped, speckled, and spotted sires. Jacob's strategy
appeared successful, but it succeeded only because it coincided with
the sovereign will of God. Genesis 30:39-42 does not imply that
Jacob's stratagems were the cause of what happened; it simply
describes what happened. In verse 42 the word translated "so" does
not necessarily imply cause and effect but simply that "it came to
pass." The word translated "rams" in the dream is more properly
"he-goats." It may be that goats, with their more striking color
variations, appeared in the dream to illustrate what would happen
with colored sires among *both* sheep and goats.

The essentials of this episode outlined above illustrate sufficiently

2. For example, Adam Clarke, C. J. Ellicott, and Franz Delitzsch.

its spiritual lessons. But the inquisitive mind will raise more far-ranging questions.

Preliminary Issues

First, is the text unquestioned? Have we got the record straight? The Syriac version has Jacob, not Laban, separate the flocks initially: "He set three days journey between himself and *Laban*" (30:36). Some commentators, including Ellicott, have favored this variant, thinking that it makes more sense out of Laban's agreement to Jacob's request. But Laban was only dealing with this request the way he had dealt with Jacob's request for Rachel's hand in marriage. The Septuagint and the Samaritan text agree with the Masoretic against the Syriac. It makes more sense that the Masoretic rendering would be changed in the direction of the Syriac rendering than vice versa, so the Masoretic must be preferred.

The textual issue leads naturally to another: What were the terms of the bargain? Jacob said, literally, "Tomorrow my righteousness shall answer for me." He evidently intended Laban to examine his herd the day after separation; from then on, Jacob would keep any animals born to his flock, irrespective of color. Laban may not have understood it this way, thinking that Jacob would keep only the off-colored animals born to his flock. At any rate, Jacob later accused Laban of changing the terms of the bargain "ten times" (31:41), trying in vain to limit the size of Jacob's herd.

Genetic Issues

A more crucial issue is the genetic one. What were the normal colors of Laban's sheep and goats? Are the specified variants recognizable today among these species, and if so, what is the pattern of their inheritance? Mammals in general have two coats of hair, the underhair which consists of numerous short, fine hairs, and the overhair, which is the one usually observed in genetic studies of coat color. In *domestic sheep*, however, the coat which has become highly developed, as a result of selection and breeding for wool, is the underhair. One should therefore remember that the coat colors observed in sheep do not strictly correspond to the coat colors of goats or other mammals.

Identification of the color variants. When animal geneticists speak of the coat color of sheep, they normally refer to the *lamb coat,* because sheep tend to change color with maturity; particularly, non-white colors become diluted—lambs born black commonly turn gray and eventually dull white. The most prevalent coat color in sheep is white, but a few breeds are typically black, or at least black-headed. Black or brown coloration is the commonest variant among white sheep, but piebald, badgerface, gray, and speckled colorations are also known.[3] Therefore, although many centuries have intervened, *the color patterns of Laban's sheep were in keeping with prevalent current patterns.* The Hebrew word for "brown" seems to imply a rich chocolate brown and is sometimes translated "black."

In his original proposal Jacob appears to allude to speckled and spotted sheep, but in the subsequent narrative, "brown" is the only deviant color he mentions specifically in connection with sheep. Therefore, it appears likely that the variants described as "striped, spotted and speckled" apply specifically to the goats.

Different breeds of goats are characterized by different colors. In general Indian and Kurdish breeds are black (although the Angora is white); Syrian breeds are generally black but sometimes piebald; Balkan and Nubian breeds are red, brown, or gray; and Alpine breeds are black and white.[4] *The color patterns of Laban's goats were in keeping with prevalent current patterns of Syrian and Kurdish goats.* This is confirmed by the fact that Laban studiously separated all the goats "that had any white in them" from Jacob's flocks.

Inheritance of coat color. To identify the color pattern of Laban's flocks is not to solve the problem of how these colors behave genetically. Whether we consider the overhair of the goat or the underhair of the sheep, the pattern of coat-color inheritance in these animals is by no means simple. Like most other genetic factors, coat color is not usually inherited in a simple Mendelian manner (fig. 1). There are several reasons for this. The coat color is determined not by just one factor but by several interacting genes, situated at different sites (loci) on the chromosomes. These loci are believed to identify stages in the biochemical process, starting with the formation of pigment cells and ending with the final pigmentation.

Even at any one locus the alternative characters (alleles) do not generally behave as simple dominants and recessives; instead partial dominance occurs, and in some cases the heterozygote has quite different characteristics from both homozygous forms.[5] Often there are not only two but several alternative (allelic) characters at one locus. Furthermore, because several interacting factors are involved, the manifestation of a particular color characteristic may be intensified, inhibited, or diluted by another factor belonging to a

3. A. L. Rae, "The Genetics of the Sheep," *Advances in Genetics* 8(1956):190-265.

4. Anthony G. Searle, *Comparative Genetics of Coat Colour in Mammals* (New York: Academic, 1968).

5. *Heterozygote* is a genetically "impure" form; that is, one with two contrasting alleles at the locus in question, one allele derived from each parent. *Homozygote* is a genetically "pure" form of gene interaction; that is, one with identical or indistinguishable alleles at the locus in question, one allele derived from each parent.

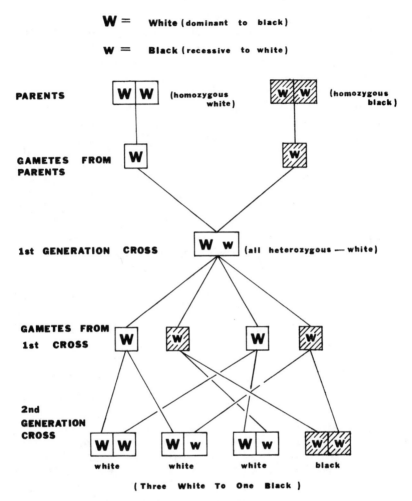

Fig. 1. Simple Mendelian inheritance illustrated

different allelic series. In breeding experiments a color is usually described as "dominant" or "recessive" depending upon the characterization of the heterozygote in crosses with animals of the standard color. The designation carries no implication that the "dominant" color variant is allelic to the standard color, or that only one gene pair is involved. A color variant may be "dominant" in breeding because it is epistatic upon other color factors.[6] The true genetic

6. *Epistasis* is a form of gene interaction whereby one gene masks or interferes with the pheonotypic expression of another nonallelic gene or genes.

interpretation of the results of breeding experiments is often difficult, and several alternative theories may be presented to explain a given result. Anomalous results which defy explanation also occur.

In the present instance we would be satisfied to know the *apparent* dominance relationship of the different colors. However, Jacob's experiments were done some 3,600 years ago, and during that time new color mutations may have been established while others disappeared. And there has been extensive migration of sheep and goats, so that the present situation may not reflect the circumstances in which Jacob's experiments occurred. The existing situation regarding color inheritance in sheep and goats is briefly outlined below.

The most common types of variant coloration in white breeds of *sheep* are black and brown, both of which are commonly recessive to white. But dominant black and dominant brown also occur.[7] Vasin reports two distinct dominant black colorations, as well as a recessive black, in Russia.[8] He proposes that recessive black occurs generally in the north and dominant black in the south, which is nearer to the upper Tigris-Euphrates valley in northern Iraq, where Laban lived.

On this basis one might guess that the chocolate brown or black coloration in Laban's sheep was *dominant* to white. If so, rams which had been born black would most often produce black lambs in the first cross with white ewes. If on the other hand black was recessive to white, then the proportion of black lambs produced by this cross would be smaller, but would depend on the number of heterozygotes among the white ewes.

In the case of *goats*, the genetics of coat-color patterns has not been studied extensively. Dominance is usually related to the agouti coloration, which is regarded as the wild type. As in the case of sheep, white appears to be generally epistatic over all other colors. Breeding experiments with the Toggenburg breed showed that black was dominant to spotting.[9] Although there is not sufficient information to warrant certainty, it is probable that the white markings which were to identify Jacob's flock would be recessive to the prevalent black or brown coloration of Laban's goats. This means that the goats that were heterozygous for spotting would not have been removed by Laban's action (because they would appear black). Hence the she-goats in Jacob's charge would produce some varicolored kids on interbreeding with varicolored sires.

On the basis of present knowledge, therefore, it is impossible to plot with certainty the course of heredity which led to the multiplica-

---

7. "Genetics of the Sheep."

8. Quoted in "Genetics of the Sheep."

9. J. L. Lush, "Inheritance of Horns, Wattles, and Colour in Grade Toggenburg Goats," *Journal of Heredity* (1926).

tion of Jacob's off-colored flocks. But it is sufficient to confirm, on the basis of well-established principles of heredity, that the influence of sires of the appropriate coloration would have the effect of greatly increasing the proportion of lambs and kids that fell to Jacob's lot.

Jacob's dream. Let us consider one final question. How did it actually occur that all the rams (or he-goats) that leaped upon the flock were of the appropriate colors, as shown to Jacob in his dream? Was this due simply to miraculous intervention? Evidently Jehovah was drawing to Jacob's attention something which Jacob had not observed. It appears that this event occurred during the autumn, when the early or "stronger" animals mated. There seems to be no need to suppose that the occurrence was repeated.

This concentration of off-colored sires could have occurred miraculously and without human intervention, either before the division of the flocks or after some of these variants had reappeared among Laban's flocks by Mendelian segregation. But it seems more in keeping with the narrative that it should have occurred through human instrumentality. Could it be that some of these separated sires somehow got among the breeding ewes and she-goats which were under Jacob's care? Could it be that Laban's own cleverness in removing the off-colored animals beforehand rebounded in this way against him?

Alternatively, it is possible that the incident occurred just after Laban had removed all varicolored animals from the flock under Jacob's care. If so, the dream implies that the dark goats which were covering the flock were *invisibly varicolored;* that is, they carried the genetic factor for the varicolored condition in a heterozygous form, which was not expressed phenotypically.[10] This would be the case if, as seems very probable, spotting was recessive to black in Laban's goats. The heterozygotes would not have been removed, and some of them would have been among the sires which covered the flock, thus ensuring some spotted kids. But it would still have to be shown why *all* the he-goats that covered the flocks in the dream were varicolored. The precise details therefore remain unknown.

Conclusions

This episode teaches some pertinent lessons. First, the scientific accuracy of the Scriptures is incidental to their spiritual purpose. Accordingly, studying them for spiritual profit yields the greatest benefits, but analyzing them scientifically may help to understand Earth history and to defend the truth.

10. F. L. Marsh, *Studies in Creationism* (Washington, D.C.: Review and Herald, 1950).

Second, although Scripture is not written in scientific form, it is in accord with true science and with contemporary knowledge in general. This is well known in the fields of archaeology, history, and physics, but less attention has been paid to this fact in biology.

Third, the concurrence of several Bible commentaries in crediting Jacob's success to prenatal influence illustrates the danger of using current science to justify Scripture, for this is to use the lesser to confirm the greater and may lead into various false accreditations of the Scriptures. We should bend neither scientific facts to conform to our interpretations of Scripture nor the Scriptures to conform to contemporary science; we should let apparent discrepancies remain as food for faith, and perhaps as matters for research. As the relevant scientific facts become well established, the Scriptures will be confirmed.

Finally, this narrative illustrates that God generally directs human affairs through responsible human actions and the timeless laws of nature, resorting to miracles only infrequently except during special periods of history. His transcendent power and wisdom are manifest in the coordination of these factors in time and space. God's normal method of operation is no less wonderful, no less divine, than His occasional miraculous interventions; both redound to the glory of the God of Jacob.

Index to Volumes 1-5

By Author

By Title